Reading Guide:

How to make your every penny investment count?

Chapters have complete configuration explained for the respective charts. So if you don't have enough time, reading the first two pages of each chapter will provide enough information to get you kick-started.

Individual charts have detailed visual explanations for graphs configurations, style, format, and recommendations. So you can also see how the final result will look and why one design is better than others for the same chart. Structured in the following order

1. **Chart Definition**
2. **Picture**
3. **Chart Data Explanation**
4. **Recommended Configurations**
5. **Other Configurations**
6. **Chart Recommendation**

For a better reading experience; following suggested

Device	App	File Format	View
iPhone	Book	ePub	Vertical Scrolling
MacBook	Book	ePub	Two Pages (Default)
MacBook	Preview	PDF	Two Pages (⌘ 3)
MacBook	Adobe Acrobat	PDF	Two Page View

iPhone Vertical Scrolling

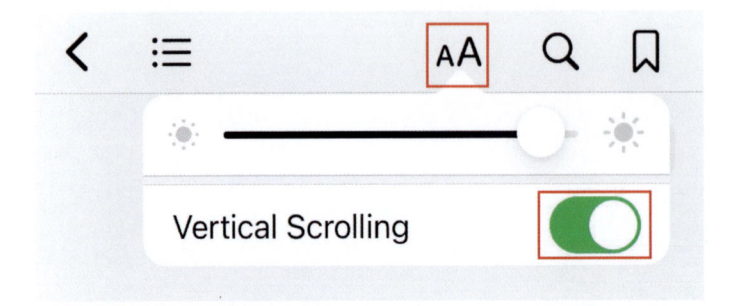

Introduction:

What would you expect to learn from this book?

With a detailed yet user-friendly guide, experts and novices alike can learn how best to utilize the extensive tools available within Google Data Studio. Create graphs, manage data and extrapolate results for presentations, reports and guides with the help of this easy-to-follow explanation.

About Author:

Deepak Kumar is an experienced Market Analyst with a background in running reports and data analysis for some of the world's biggest brands. Across an international career he's worked with leading researchers, strategists and company directors to help organizations gain meaningful insights and actionable knowledge that consistently drives companies forward.

Not a native English speaker; please excuse some grammatical errors.

Data Visualization:

Why do we need data visualization?

Right now, Data Visualization is a hot commodity. Whether you're a small business owner looking to create financial reports or a PhD student finalizing an important piece of research, it's vital to make sure the charts and graphs you use to display data are clear, easy to understand and visually appealing.

It's no longer enough to simply visually display data in complex, hard to read spreadsheets. Properly visualized data is easy to understand for all of your audiences and can help make important trends clear. From this, analytics and full guides can be created, appealing to everyone from the CEO right through to your day-to-day clients or other stakeholders.

However you intend to use it, it's more important than ever that you understand Data Visualization, and this is the guide to help.

Why use Google Data Studio - brings your data to life

- Google Data Studio is the tool to bring your data to life. Bring in figures and research from multiple sources across the internet, including social networking sites such as Facebook and Twitter.

- It's also the tool to help transform this information. Easy to use yet sufficiently advanced for professional level reporting, Google Data Studio allows you to tell stories with your information – including high-level reports and easy-to-update digital dashboards.

- Finally, Google Data Studio allows you and your audiences to gain meaningful insights from raw data. From this, the conclusions you draw will create genuine action for your organization.

Chapter 1: Configuration Across Charts 8
    I. Background and Border — all Charts 8
    II. Missing Data 9
    III. Conditional Formatting 10
    IV. Chart Header — All Charts 12
    V. Legends 13
    VI. Reference Lines 14

Chapter 2: Scorecards 16
    I. Scorecards: Raw Number 18
    II. Scorecards: Compact Number 20
    III. Scorecard: For % DATA 22
    IV. How To Create a Unified Scorecard 24
    V. Padding and Line Height 25

Chapter 3: Pie/Doughnut Charts 26
    I. Pie Chart 28
    II. Doughnut Chart 30
    III. Pie/Doughnut Chart With Value as a Data Label 32
    IV. Column/Bar Chart as a Pie/Doughnut Chart Alternative 33

Chapter 4: Bullet Charts 34
    I. Bullet Chart: With Target and Ranges 36
    II. Bullet Chart: Without Target (Ranges Only) 38
    III. Bullet Chart: With Target Ranges and Comparison 40

Chapter 5: Gauge Charts 42
    I. Default Gauge Chart 44
    II. Gauge Chart With Target Only 46
    III. Gauge Chart With Ranges Only (Without Target) 48
    IV. Gauge Chart With Target and Comparison 50

Chapter 6: Line Charts/Time Series Charts 52
    I. Line Chart: Double Axis 54
    II. Line Chart: Single Axis 56
    III. Sparkline Chart: 58
    IV. How Are Sparkline Charts Often Used? 58
    V. Smoothed Time Series Chart: 59

Chapter 7: Column Charts 60
    I. Column Chart: Single Axis 62
    II. Column Chart With Multiple Metrics: Single Axis 64
    III. Column Chart: Dual Axis (1/2) 66
    IV. Column Chart: Dual Axis (2/2) 68

- V. Stacked Column: Single Axis 70
- VI. Stacked Column: Dual Axis 72
- VII. 100% Stacked Column (1/2) 74
- VIII. 100% Stacked Column (2/2) 76

Chapter 8: Combo Charts 78
- I. Combo Chart: Double Axis 80
- II. Combo Chart: Single Axis 82
- III. Stacked Combo Chart: Single Axis 84
- IV. Stacked Combo Chart: Dual Axis 86

Chapter 9: Table 88
- I. Table 90
- II. Table With Bars 92
- III. Table With Heatmap 94
- IV. RAW Data Table 96

Chapter 10: Pivot Tables 98
- I. Pivot Table 100
- II. Pivot Table With Bars 102
- III. Pivot Table With Heatmap 104
- IV. Pivot Table With Bars: With "Expand – Collapse" Option 106

Chapter 11: Area Charts 108
- I. Area Chart 110
- II. 100% Stacked Area Chart 112
- III. Area Chart: Show Stack 114

Chapter 12: Scatter Charts 116
- I. Scatter Chart 118
- II. Scatter Chart: Two or More Dimensions 120

Chapter 13: Bubble Chart = Scatter Chart + Bubble Size 122
- I. Bubble Chart = Scatter Chart + Bubble Size Configuration 124
- II. Bubble Chart: Two or More Dimensions 126

Chapter 14: Geo Maps Charts 128
- I. Geo Chart 130
- II. Filled Map 132
- III. Bubble Map 134

Chapter 15: Treemap 136
- I. Treemap Chart 137
- II. Treemap Chart – Two or More Dimension 138

Chapter 1: Configuration Across Charts

I. Background and Border – All Charts

Background and Border offer ways to customize the appearance of charts individually or on the report level. For instance, you may want to customize your charts to match your company branding color. Consistent and meaningful use of color makes your reports more attractive and easier to understand. You can apply color and border options to every available chart in Google Data Studio. If you are unsure about a uniform design, please use the standard design available in Google Data Studio. The color and style settings of these design are set so that the reports are visually appealing and suitable for color-blind users.

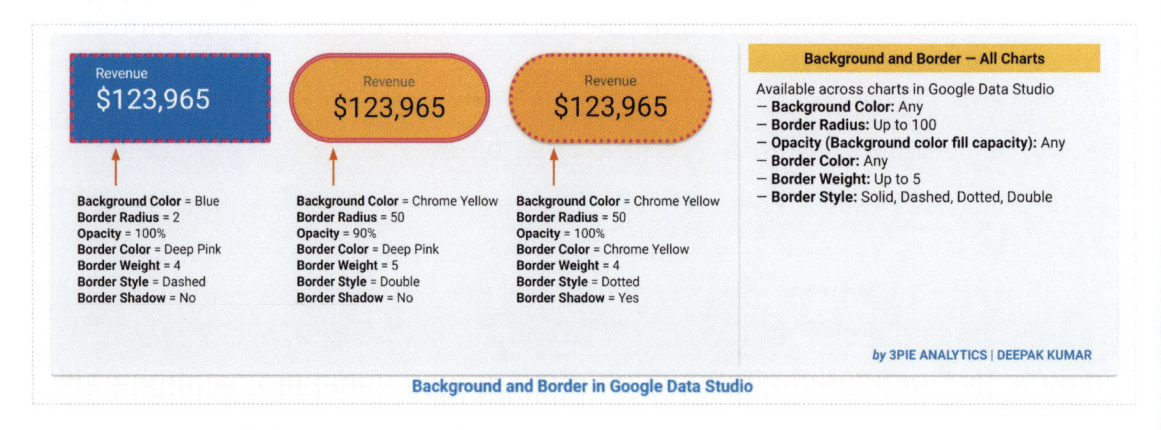

Background and Border — All Charts

Available across charts in Google Data Studio
- Background Color: Any
- Border Radius: Up to 100
- Opacity (Background color fill capacity): Any
- Border Color: Any
- Border Weight: Up to 5
- Border Style: Solid, Dashed, Dotted, Double

Revenue $123,965
Background Color = Blue
Border Radius = 2
Opacity = 100%
Border Color = Deep Pink
Border Weight = 4
Border Style = Dashed
Border Shadow = No

Revenue $123,965
Background Color = Chrome Yellow
Border Radius = 50
Opacity = 90%
Border Color = Deep Pink
Border Weight = 5
Border Style = Double
Border Shadow = No

Revenue $123,965
Background Color = Chrome Yellow
Border Radius = 50
Opacity = 100%
Border Color = Chrome Yellow
Border Weight = 4
Border Style = Dotted
Border Shadow = Yes

Background and Border in Google Data Studio

by 3PIE ANALYTICS | DEEPAK KUMAR

Available across charts in Google Data Studio

Configuration	Options
Background Color	Any
Border Radius	Up to 100
Opacity (Background color fill capacity)	0-100%
Border Color	Any
Border Weight	Up to 5
Border Style	Solid, Dashed, Dotted, Double

II. Missing Data

This option controls how to display missing values according to your preference. For example, when data is missing from the scorecard, you can choose to show blanks, 0 (Zero), hyphens, the words "null or "No data."

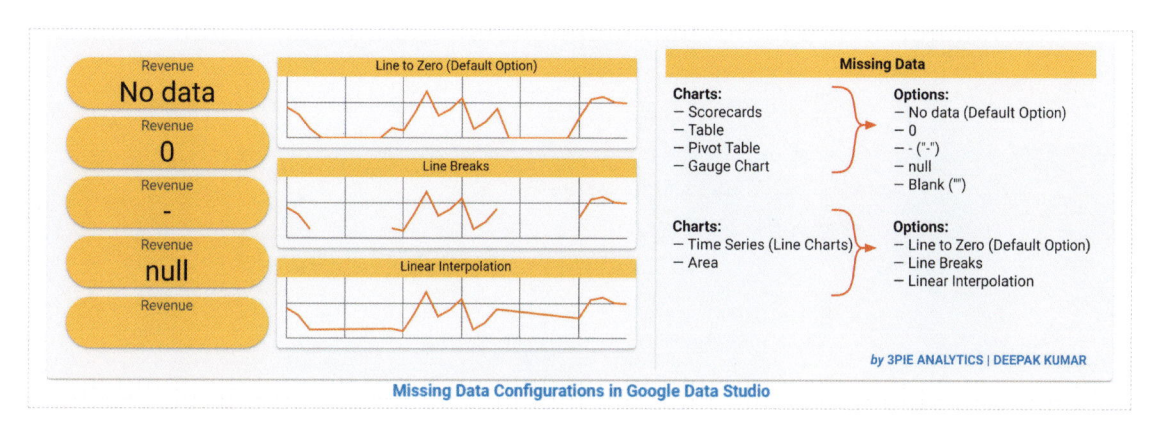

Missing Data Configurations in Google Data Studio

[Missing Data] – options include "null", 0, - ("-"), "No data", and "" (Blank) for following charts
– **Scorecards** – **Table** – **Pivot Table** – **Gauge Chart**

[Missing Data] – three options including "Line to zero" (Default Option), "Line breaks", and "Linear Interpolation" for the following charts
– **Time Series** – **Area**

Page 9

III. Conditional Formatting

Based on the data, you can set the font and background colors used in your charts. For example, if Revenue is greater than 1000, then set the scorecard background color to green.

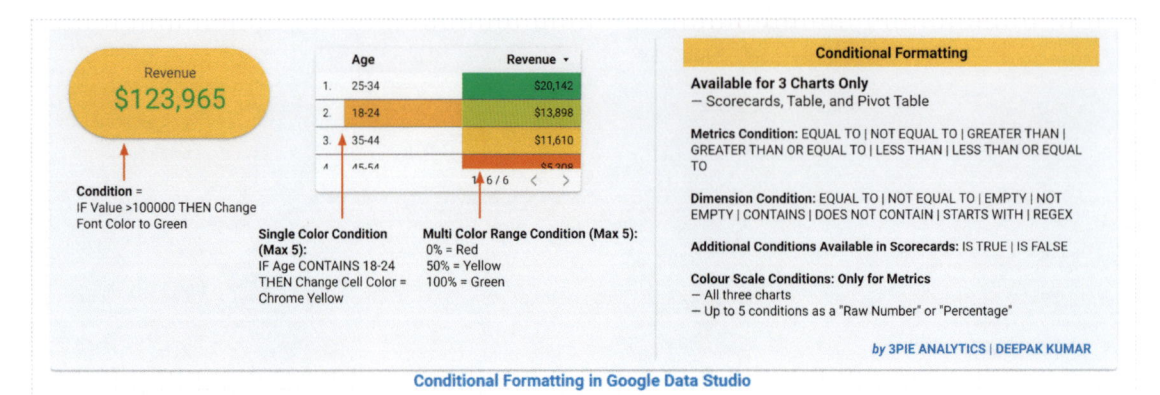

Conditional Formatting in Google Data Studio

Conditional formatting only available within 3 charts

- **Scorecards**
- **Table**
- **Pivot Table**

Metrics condition:

EQUAL TO | NOT EQUAL TO | GREATER THAN | GREATER THAN OR EQUAL TO | LESS THAN | LESS THAN OR EQUAL TO | EMPTY | NOT EMPTY | IS TRUE | IS FALSE | CONTAINS | DOES NOT CONTAIN | STARTS WITH | REGEX

Dimensions condition:

EQUAL TO | NOT EQUAL TO | EMPTY | NOT EMPTY | CONTAINS | DOES NOT CONTAIN | STARTS WITH | REGEX | IS FALSE | CONTAINS | DOES NOT CONTAIN | STARTS WITH | REGEX

Additional conditions available in Scorecard

IS TRUE | IS FLASE

Single color conditional formatting

Single color conditional formatting lets you apply a specific font color and background to your data. Single color conditions can include:
- Dimensions
- Metrics
- Multiple conditions using AND/OR logic.

Color scale conditional formatting

Color scale conditions let you evaluate a single metric against its percentage or absolute numeric value.

How to select colors?
- Hover over an existing data point and click Add icon to add more data points.
- To remove a data point, hover over it and click the Delete icon.

Single color: Use the color pickers to select the font color and background color to the target values for each condition. You'll see an example appear on the right.

Color scale: The data points determine your color scale's minimum, middle, and maximum values . By default, the new color scale defines 3 data points by percentage with preset colors (red, yellow, green). However, you can base the scale on whole numbers and choose a different color for each data point.

Conditional formatting limitation
- You can have a maximum of 5 data points and a minimum of 2 data points.
- Solid color conditional formatting is currently only available for tables, pivot tables, and scorecards.
- Color scale conditional formatting is currently available for tables and scorecards.
- Conditional formatting on pivot tables that use Expand-Collapse only works if the rule is based on "Any value."
- Dimension-based compound conditions in pivot tables must use the same field in each OR condition.
- Format rules can only use fields currently contained in the chart.
- A maximum of 20 formatting rules can be set per chart.
- Switching between chart visualization types (for example, switching a table to a scorecard) may require you to update conditional formatting rules, depending on the type of chart and the fields used in the rule.

IV. Chart Header – All Charts

Chart headers allow viewers to perform several actions on charts, such as data export, drilling up or down, and view charts in explorer tools. Available across charts in Google Data Studio and the color is also customizable.

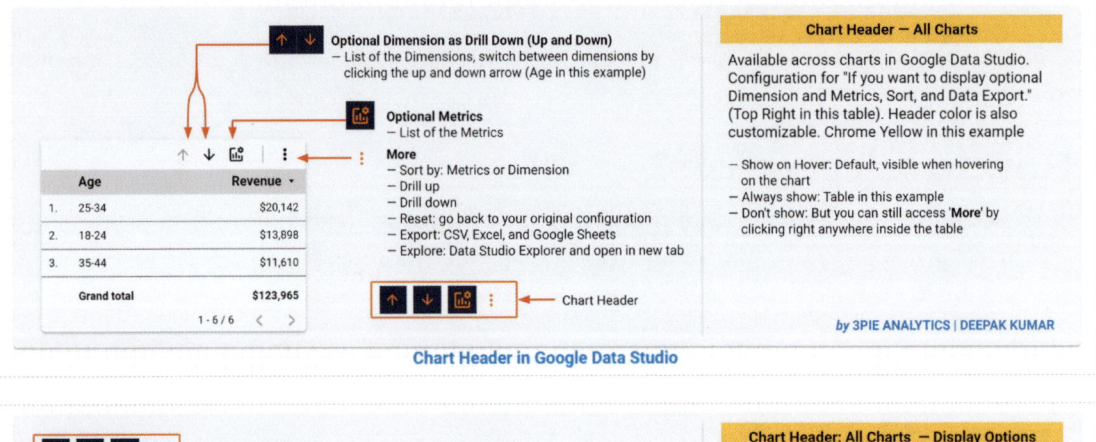

Chart Header in Google Data Studio

Optional Dimension as Drill Down (Up and Down)
— List of the Dimensions, switch between dimensions by clicking the up and down arrow (Age in this example)

Optional Metrics
— List of the Metrics

More
— Sort by: Metrics or Dimension
— Drill up
— Drill down
— Reset: go back to your original configuration
— Export: CSV, Excel, and Google Sheets
— Explore: Data Studio Explorer and open in new tab

Chart Header — All Charts
Available across charts in Google Data Studio. Configuration for "If you want to display optional Dimension and Metrics, Sort, and Data Export." (Top Right in this table). Header color is also customizable. Chrome Yellow in this example

— Show on Hover: Default, visible when hovering on the chart
— Always show: Table in this example
— Don't show: But you can still access '**More**' by clicking right anywhere inside the table

by 3PIE ANALYTICS | DEEPAK KUMAR

Chart Header (Display Options) in Google Data Studio

Chart Header: Always show

Chart Header: Show on hover (Default) — Chart header will appear once you hover the mouse anywhere inside the chart

Chart Header: Do not show

Chart Header: All Charts — Display Options
— Always show: Table in this example
— Show on Hover: Default, visible when hovering on the chart
— Don't show: But you can still access **More** by clicking right anywhere inside the table

↑ ↓ Optional Dimension as Drill Down (Up and Down)
      Optional Metrics
  ⋮   More

by 3PIE ANALYTICS | DEEPAK KUMAR

Display Options:	
Always show	Header options are always visible. Table 1 in the above picture.
Show on hover (default)	Hovering over the chart header shows three vertical dots. Click to access the header options. Table 2 in the picture
Don't show	Header options do not appear. However, report viewers can always access the options by right-clicking the chart. Table 3 in the above picture.

V. Legends

These options decide the placement and visibility of the chart legend. Legend Alignment and Max lines are also configurable.

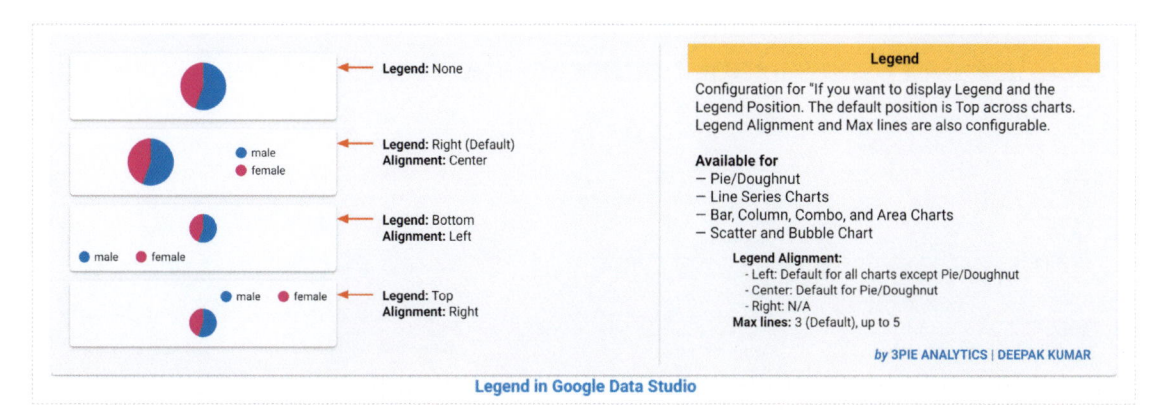

Legend in Google Data Studio

Available for following charts:
− Pie/Doughnut
− Line Series Charts
− Bar, Column, Combo, and Area Charts
− Scatter and Bubble Chart

Display Options:	
None	No legend appears
Right	Legend appears on the right.
Bottom	Legend appears on the bottom.
Top	Legend appears on the top
Alignment	Sets the alignment of the legend relative to the selected position.
Max lines	Sets the number of lines used by the legend. If the number of series requires more lines, hidden items can be displayed by clicking the < and > arrows.

VI. Reference Lines

Reference lines show how the data in a chart compares to a reference value or let you show target values and set thresholds and benchmarks. For example, you can use reference lines to visualize daily sales against a target sales figure.

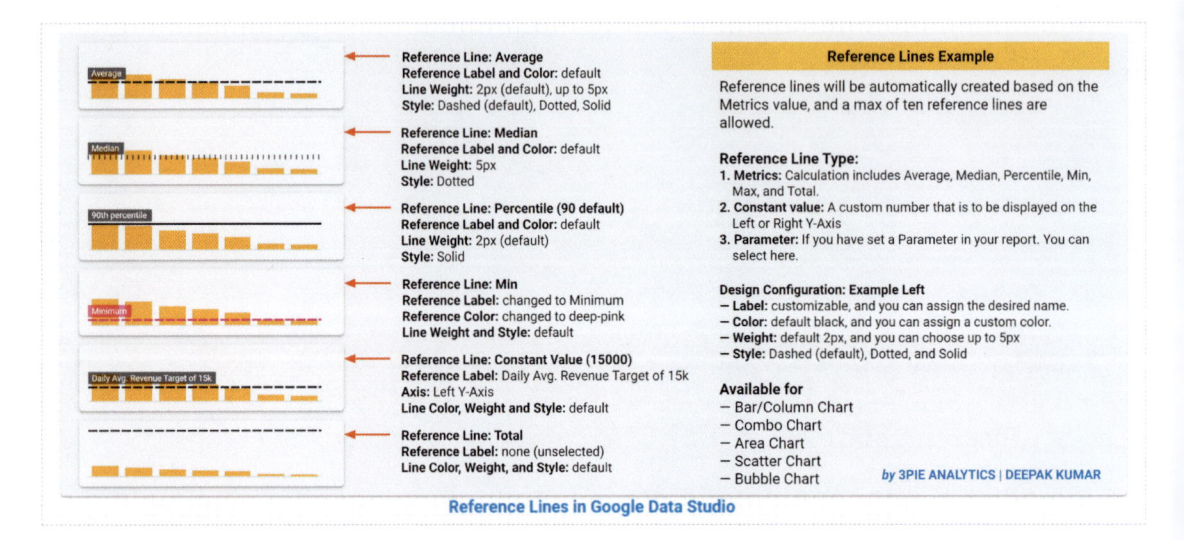

Reference Line: Average **Reference Label and Color:** default **Line Weight:** 2px (default), up to 5px **Style:** Dashed (default), Dotted, Solid	**Reference Lines Example** Reference lines will be automatically created based on the Metrics value, and a max of ten reference lines are allowed.
Reference Line: Median **Reference Label and Color:** default **Line Weight:** 5px **Style:** Dotted	**Reference Line Type:** 1. **Metrics:** Calculation includes Average, Median, Percentile, Min, Max, and Total. 2. **Constant value:** A custom number that is to be displayed on the Left or Right Y-Axis 3. **Parameter:** If you have set a Parameter in your report. You can select here.
Reference Line: Percentile (90 default) **Reference Label and Color:** default **Line Weight:** 2px (default) **Style:** Solid	
Reference Line: Min **Reference Label:** changed to Minimum **Reference Color:** changed to deep-pink **Line Weight and Style:** default	**Design Configuration: Example Left** — **Label:** customizable, and you can assign the desired name. — **Color:** default black, and you can assign a custom color. — **Weight:** default 2px, and you can choose up to 5px — **Style:** Dashed (default), Dotted, and Solid
Reference Line: Constant Value (15000) **Reference Label:** Daily Avg. Revenue Target of 15k **Axis:** Left Y-Axis **Line Color, Weight and Style:** default	**Available for** — Bar/Column Chart — Combo Chart — Area Chart — Scatter Chart — Bubble Chart
Reference Line: Total **Reference Label:** none (unselected) **Line Color, Weight, and Style:** default	*by 3PIE ANALYTICS	DEEPAK KUMAR*

Reference Lines in Google Data Studio

Reference Line Type:
Metrics: Calculation includes Average, Median, Percentile, Min, Max, and
Constant value: A custom number that is to be displayed on the Left or Right Y-Axis
Parameter: If you have set a Parameter in your report. You can select here.
Available for following charts:

— Line/Time Series
   — Bar/Column Chart
   — Combo Chart
   — Area Chart
   — Scatter Chart
   — Bubble Chart

Editing Charts with Reference Lines

- Changing the chart type will delete any reference lines not supported by the new chart type—for example, Line Chart to Scorecard.
- If you remove a metric from the chart, it will delete any reference lines associated with that metric.

Reference Lines Limitation

- Reference lines are only available for numeric axes. Reference lines on date axes aren't supported.
- Metric-based reference lines can only consider values currently displayed in the chart. So, for example, if you add a reference line to a bar chart with 10 bars, data from additional bars is not included in the calculation.
- It is not possible to insert reference lines in 100% stacked charts.
- Only constant values and parameters reference lines are supported in Stacked column, stacked bar, and stacked area charts.

Trendlines:

Trend lines reveal the general tendency of the data on a chart. Trend lines allow you to spot patterns and make predictions from otherwise random data. You can add trend lines to time series and scatter charts.

Trendline Types

1. **Linear:** Linear trend lines are straight lines that approximate the data on the chart as closely as possible.
2. **Exponential:** You can use an exponential trendline when an exponential of the form e^{ax+b} best represents your data.
3. **Polynomial:** A polynomial trendline displays data directionality as a curved line. It can help analyze large, highly variable data series.

Chapter 2: Scorecards

Scorecards display a summary of a single metric and are the most commonly used way to visualize core key performance indicators (KPIs).

Use case:

1. **Scorecards with Raw Number** – for reports with figures within five digits or those that contain sensitive numerical data (such as prices or sales).
2. **Scorecards with a Compact Number** – if your numbers are more than five digits and are not sensitive like Sessions and Page Views.
3. **Scorecards for % Data** – only with absolute changes configuration
4. **Unified Scorecards** – with this format, you can display both "% Changes" and "Absolute Change" for KPIs.

Recommended:

Yes, especially if you intend to make a report for senior management personnel, it's highly recommended to display core KPI performance changes.

Scorecards in Google Data Studio				
Chart Type	Date Type	Changes	Recommended	Unified Scorecards
Scorecards: Raw Number	Sensitive	Both, Absolute and % Changes	Yes	Yes
Scorecards: Compact Number	Non-sensitive	Both, Absolute and % Changes	Yes	Yes
Scorecard: for % data	%	Absolute Changes	Yes	No

Recommended Configurations For Scorecards:

1. **[Metric Name]** – you should also always display the metric name.
2. **[Comparison]** – in the Scorecard, you should always display the Comparison.
3. **[Comparison Label]** – only to be used if individual charts on the page/report have multiple date range comparisons. For instance, if your page has the same comparison level across KPIs, you can put a remark at the bottom of the page, such as: "On this page, changes are from the previous period."

4. **[Comparison Metric Color]** – this can be customized to display the 'Increase' or 'Decrease' value in different colors; for instance, **green to display a decrease in Bounce Rate or Negative Sentiment**.
5. **[Remark]** – add a remark on the bottom right corner of a scorecard (for example, Chart B) displaying the absolute change. This way, the report audience can quickly identify the "Absolute Change" and "% Change data".
6. **[Conditional Formatting]** – please refer to page 10 for a detailed explanation.

Other Configurations Available Within Scorecard:

7. **[Missing Data]** – at default this will show as "No data". Other options include: 0, - ("-"), null, and Blank (""). Please refer to page 9 for a detailed explanation.
8. **[Compact Numbers and Decimal Precision]** – default, unselected with auto decimal precision
9. **[Hide Metric Name]** – default unselected
10. **[Font Color, Size, and Family]** – individually customizable
11. **[Alignment]** – default is left, but this can be customized individually to Middle or Right for Metric Name, Value and Comparison.
12. **[Background Color, Border Radius and Opacity]** – customizable; please refer to page 8 for a detailed explanation.
13. **[Border Color, Weight, Style, and Shadow]** – customizable; please refer to page 8 for a detailed explanation.
14. **[Line Height]** – please leave to default auto; this might condense two rows of data in one. PDF export will also result in a messy, disorganized result. An example is shown on page 25.
15. **[Padding]** – reserved space for Left, Right, and Top. An example is shown on page 25.
16. **[Chart Header and Font Color]** – chart headers allow viewers to perform several actions on charts, such as data export, drilling up or down, and view charts in explorer tools. Please refer to page 11 for a detailed explanation.

I. Scorecards: Raw Number

For reports with figures within five digits or those that contain sensitive numerical data (such as prices or sales)

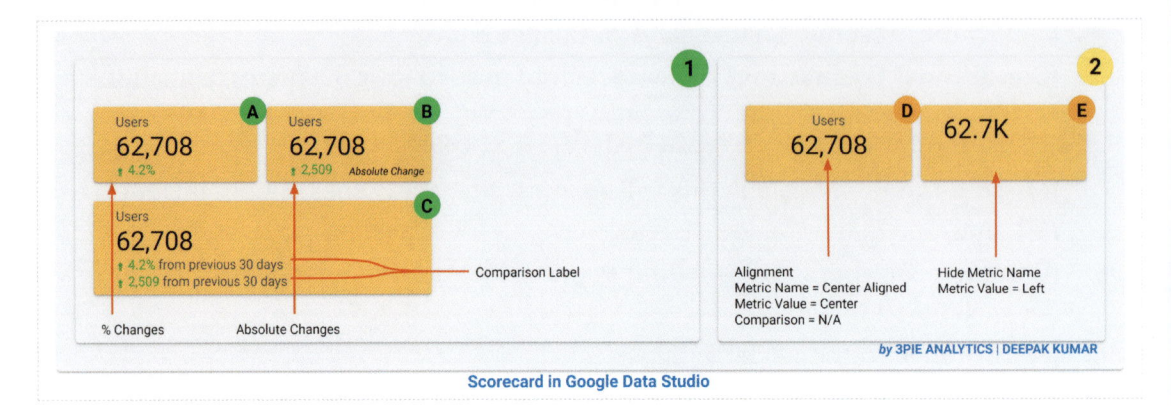

Scorecard in Google Data Studio

– Above, we have five types of Scorecards: Scorecard A, showing % Change; B, showing absolute change; Chart C, a unified scorecard displaying % Change and Absolute Change; Chart D, displaying an absolute number without Comparison and finally Chart E, showing the compact number without Comparison and Metric.

Chart Configurations:

1. **[Unified Scorecard]** – a personal favorite, displaying both "% Change" and "Absolute change", Chart C in this example
2. **[Metric Name]** – you should also always display the metric name. In the above example, this is 'Users'.
3. **[Comparison]** – in the Scorecard, you should always display the Comparison. "from previous 30 days" in this example
4. **[Comparison Label]** – ("from previous 30 days" Chart C in this example): Only to be used if individual charts on the page/report have multiple date range comparisons. For instance, if your page has the same comparison level across KPIs, you can put a remark at the bottom of the page, such as: "On this page, changes are from the previous period."
5. **[Remark]** – add a remark on the bottom right corner of a scorecard (for example, Chart B) displaying the absolute change. This way, the report audience can quickly identify the "Absolute Change" and "% Change data".
6. **[Compact Numbers]** – selected for Chart E in this example
7. **[Show Absolute Change]** – configured in the STYLE tab and selected for Chart B in this example
8. **[Font Color]** – in this Scorecard this is default Black.
9. **[Font Family and Size]** – Roboto 28 in the above Scorecard - the theme default. The minimum size is 8, while the maximum is 98.

Page 18

10. **[Hide Metric Name]** – you can also hide the Metric name - 'Users', Chart E in this example.
11. **[Alignment]** – default is left, but this can be customized individually to Middle (Chart D) or Right for Metric Name, Value and Comparison.
12. **[Background Color]** – chrome yellow in the above Scorecard, but default will depend on how you have set up your theme.
13. **[Border Radius]** – 4 in this example
14. **[Border Color]** – transparent in this Scorecard and default will depend on how you have set up your theme.
15. **[Border Shadow]** – "Add Border Shadow" selected for this example

Other Configurations: Left To Default

16. **[Conditional Formatting]** – none, please refer to page 10 for a detailed explanation.
17. **[Decimal Precision]** – auto
18. **[Missing Data]** – default "No data." Please refer to page 9 for a detailed explanation.
19. **[Comparison Metric Color]** – default is green for the increase and red for a decrease
20. **[Background Opacity]** – 100%
21. **[Border Weight and Style]** – none
22. **[Line Height]** – auto
23. **[Padding]** – default, Left 24px, Right 24px, and Top 8px
24. **[Chart Header and Font Color]** – chart headers allow viewers to perform several actions on charts, such as data export, drilling up or down, and view charts in explorer tools. Please refer to page 12 for a detailed explanation.

Recommended: Yes [A, B, Or C]

- For reports with figures within five digits or those that contain sensitive numerical data (such as prices or sales)
- For reports intended for senior management personnel, it's highly recommended to display core KPI performance changes.

II. Scorecards: Compact Number

For reports with figures more than five digits or those that contain non-sensitive numerical data (Sessions or Pageviews)

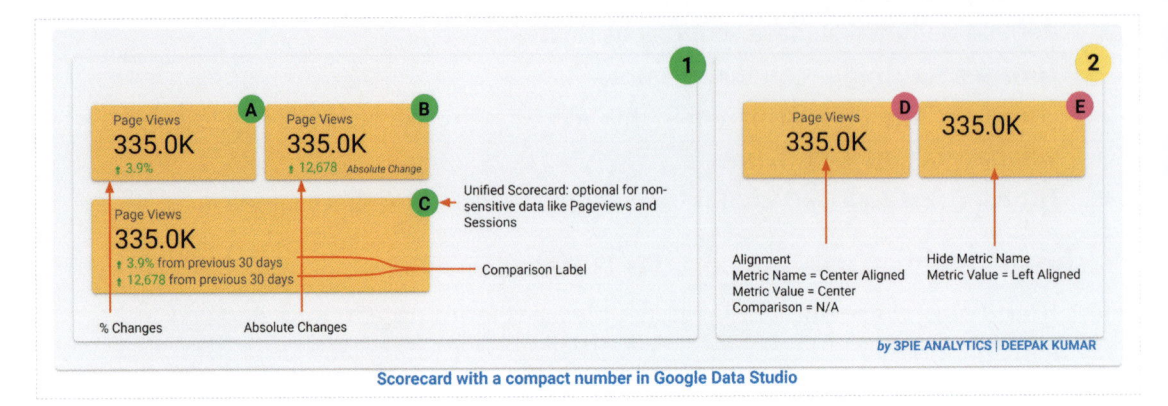

Scorecard with a compact number in Google Data Studio

— Above, we have five types of charts: Scorecard A, with % Change; B, with Absolute Change; C, a unified scorecard displaying % Change and Absolute Change; D, showing Absolute Number without comparison and Scorecard E, compact number and 0 decimal precision without comparison.

Chart Configurations:

1. **[Unified Scorecard]** – optional for non-sensitive data such as Page Views and Sessions
2. **[Compact Number]** – selected in this example
3. **[Metric Name]** – you should also always display the metric name. In the above example, this is 'Users'.
4. **[Comparison]** – in the Scorecard, if your data set allows, you should always display the Comparison. "from previous 30 days" in this example.
5. **[Comparison Label]** – ("from previous 30 days" Chart C in this example): Only to be used if individual charts on the page/report have multiple date range comparisons. For instance, if your page has the same comparison level across KPIs, you can put a remark at the bottom of the page, such as: "On this page, changes are from the previous period."
6. **[Remark]** – add a remark on the bottom right corner of a scorecard (for example, Chart B) displaying the absolute change. This way, the report audience can quickly identify the Absolute Change and % Change data.
7. **[Compact Numbers]** – selected in this example
8. **[Show Absolute Change]** – configured in the STYLE tab and selected for Chart B in this example
9. **[Font Color]** – default black.

Page 20

10. **[Font Family and Size]** – Roboto 28 in the above Scorecard - the theme default. The minimum size is 8, while the maximum is 98.
11. **[Hide Metric Name]** – you can also hide the Metric name - 'Users', Chart E in this example.
12. **[Alignment]** – default is left, but this can be customized individually to Middle (Chart D) or Right for Metric Name, Value and Comparison.
13. **[Background Color]** – Chrome yellow in the above Scorecard, but default will depend on how you have set up your theme.
14. **[Border Radius]** – 4 in this example
15. **[Border Color]** – transparent in this Scorecard and default will depend on how you have set up your theme.
16. **[Border Shadow]** – "Add Border Shadow" selected for this example

Other Configurations: Left To Default

17. **[Conditional Formatting]** – none
18. **[Decimal Precision]** – auto
19. **[Missing Data]** – default "No data." Please refer to page 9 for a detailed explanation.
20. **[Comparison Metric Color]** – default is **green for the increase** and **red for a decrease**
21. **[Background Opacity]** – 100%
22. **[Border Weight and Style]** – none
23. **[Line Height]** – auto
24. **[Padding]** – default, Left 24px, Right 24px, and Top 8px
25. **[Chart Header and Font Color]** – chart headers allow viewers to perform several actions on charts, such as data export, drilling up or down, and view charts in explorer tools. Please refer to page 12 for a detailed explanation.

Recommended: Yes [A, B, Or C]

- Yes, if your numbers are more than five digits and are not sensitive like Sessions and Page Views.
- Especially if you intend to make a report for senior management personnel, it's highly recommended to display core KPI performance changes.

III. Scorecard: for % DATA

Only with absolute changes configuration

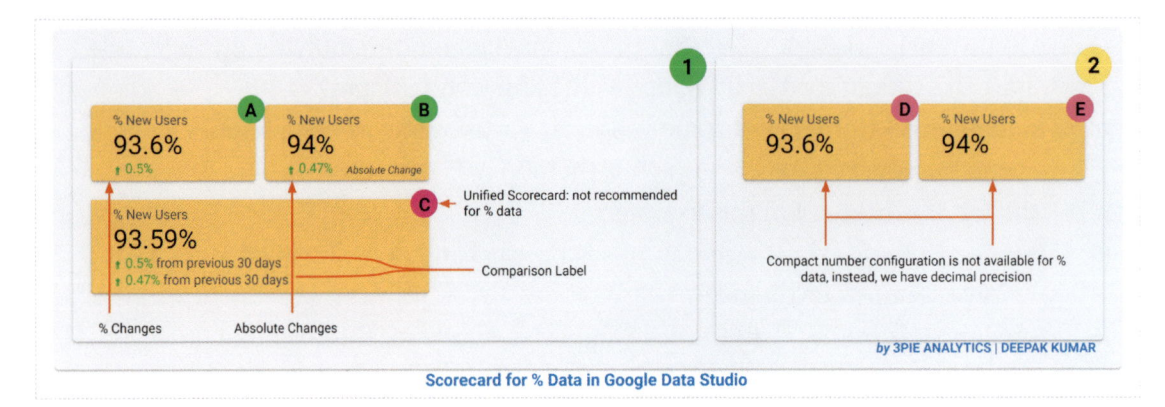

Scorecard for % Data in Google Data Studio

- Above, we have five types of charts: Scorecard A, showing % Change; B, displaying absolute change; C, a unified scorecard displaying % Change and Absolute Change; D, without decimal precision and without comparison, and E, with 0 decimal precision without comparison. Let's explore how changes are calculated in Scorecard A and B and to see if we can quickly figure out the old data (93.12%) from 93.59%

In Chart A, we have 0.5% which is calculated as:

% Change = new value/old value-1

In Chart B, we have 0.47%, which is calculated as:

Absolute Change = new value - old value

As you can see, it's easier to add or subtract than to calculate a % change. Therefore, for any % data, the best practice is to use absolute changes for comparison.

Chart Configurations:

1. **[Unified Scorecard]** – not recommended for % data
2. **[Metric Name]** – you should also always display the metric name. In the above example, this is 'Users'.
3. **[Comparison]** – in the Scorecard, if your data set allows, you should always display the Comparison. "from previous 30 days" in this example.
4. **[Comparison Label]** – ("from previous 30 days" Chart C in this example): Only to be used if individual charts on the page/report have multiple date range comparisons. For instance, if your page has the same comparison level across KPIs, you can put a remark at the bottom of the page, such as: "On this page, changes are from the previous period."

5. **[Remark]** – add a remark on the bottom right corner of a scorecard (for example, Chart B) displaying the absolute change. This way, the report audience can quickly identify the Absolute Change and % Change data.
6. **[Compact Numbers]** – selected for Scorecard E in this example
7. **[Show Absolute Change]** – configured in the STYLE tab and selected for Chart B in this example
8. **[Font Color]** – default black.
9. **[Font Family and Size]** – Roboto 28 in the above Scorecard - the theme default. The minimum size is 8, while the maximum is 98.
10. **[Hide Metric Name]** – you can also hide the Metric name - 'Users', Chart E in this example.
11. **[Alignment]** – default is left, but this can be customized individually to Middle (Chart D) or Right for Metric Name, Value and Comparison.
12. **[Background Color]** – Chrome yellow in the above Scorecard, but default will depend on how you have set up your theme.
13. **[Border Radius]** – 4 in this example
14. **[Border Color]** – transparent in this Scorecard and default will depend on how you have set up your theme.
15. **[Border Shadow]** – "Add Border Shadow" selected for this example

Other Configurations: Left To Default

16. **[Conditional Formatting]** – none, please refer to page 10 for a detailed explanation.
17. **[Decimal Precision]** – auto
18. **[Missing Data]** – default "No data." Please refer to page 9 for a detailed explanation.
19. **[Comparison Metric Color]** – default is **green for the increase** and **red for a decrease**
20. **[Background Opacity]** – 100%
21. **[Border Weight and Style]** – none
22. **[Line Height]** – auto
23. **[Padding]** – default, Left 24px, Right 24px, and Top 8px
24. **[Chart Header and Font Color]** – chart headers allow viewers to perform several actions on charts, such as data export, drilling up or down, and view charts in explorer tools. Please refer to page 12 for a detailed explanation.

Recommended: Yes [A, B Or C]

- Yes, and only with absolute changes (Scorecard B) configuration for all % data

IV. How to create a Unified Scorecard

Stacked on top of each other to display unified absolute changes and % changes in a scorecard. Create scorecard in 3,2,1 order (3rd scorecard first) to avoid manually arranging stacking order.

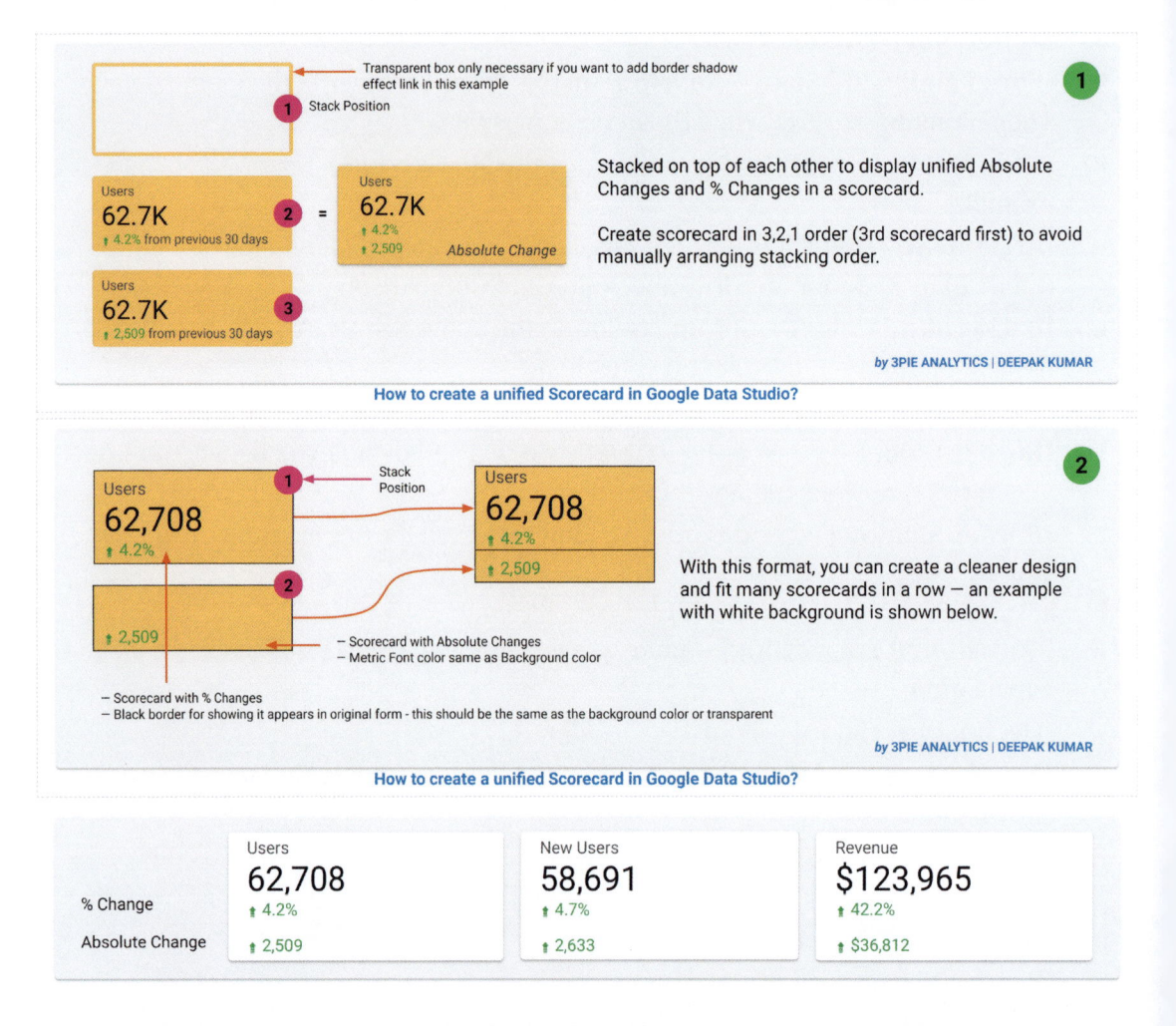

- With this format, you can display both % Changes and Absolute Change for KPIs, create a cleaner design, and fit many scorecards in a row.

Recommended: Yes

- My personal favorite, depending on the dashboard format and design. I have used one of two formats for every dashboard I have built.

Page 24

V. Padding and Line Height

1. **Padding: Reserved space for Left, Right, and Top shown in the below example.**
2. **Line Height: Space between rows in pixels. Please leave to default auto; this might condense two rows of data in one. PDF export will also result in a messy, disorganized result.**

Scorecard Padding and Line Height in Google Data Studio

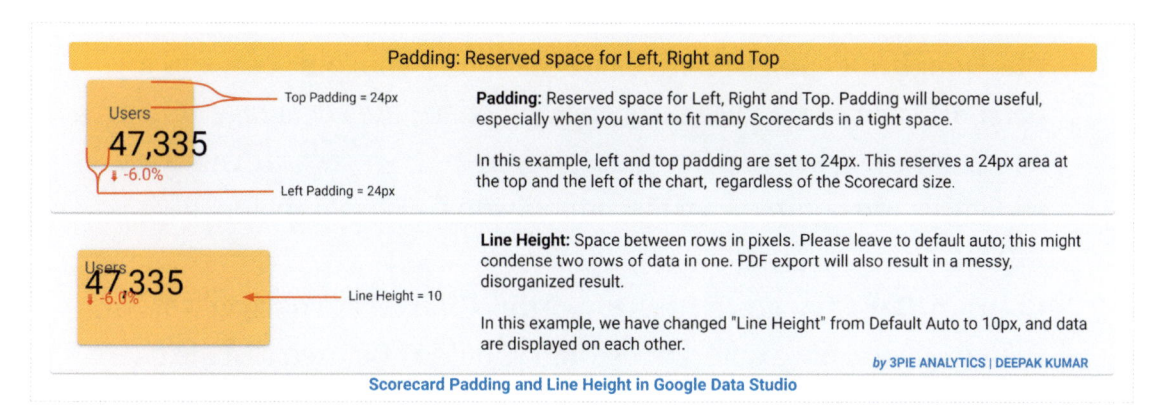

Chart Configurations:

1. **Padding:** in the first Scorecard, the Left and Top have a 24px reserve area regardless of the Scorecard size. This will become useful, especially when you want to fit many scorecards in a tight space
2. **Line Height:** in the second Scorecard, we have changed "Line Height" from Default Auto to 10px, and data are displayed on each other.

Recommended: Yes, On A Particular Case

- **Padding:** Yes, but only in the particular case when you have to fit many scorecards in a tight space.
- **Line Height:** Please leave to default auto; this might condense two rows of data in one. PDF export will also result in a messy, disorganized result.

Chapter 3: Pie/Doughnut Charts

A Pie/Doughnut chart expresses a part-to-whole relationship in a data set. It will always add up to 100%. So, if, for instance, you want to show "How does 100% divide up into multiple shares?" you should always use a Pie/Doughnut Chart with % as a data label.

Use case:

1. **Pie/Doughnut Charts:** both charts have the same purpose, and my personal favorite is to use the Doughnut chart; the advantage of using a doughnut chart has a space in the middle for a Scorecard. This way, audiences can compare against an individual element that makes up 100%.
2. **Column/Bar Chart as a Pie/Doughnut Chart Alternative:** No, Bar/Column charts have different use and shouldn't be used as a Pie chart alternative.

Recommended:

Yes, this is one of the most widely used charts across the industry.

Pie/Doughnut Chart in Google Data Studio				
Chart Type	Data Labels	Legend	Recommended
Pie Chart	Always %	Always	Yes
Doughnut Chart	Always %	Always	Yes (Personal Favorite)
Column/Bar Chart as an alternative?	No, Bar/Column charts have different use and shouldn't be used as a Pie chart alternative.		

Recommended Configurations For Pie/Doughnut Charts:

1. **[Chart Title]** – unlike a Scorecard, a Pie chart doesn't have a Metric name. A best practice is to add a chart title so audiences can see metrics used in the chart.
2. **[Pie Slices/Number of Slices]** – default is 10, while the maximum number is 20. You should test for the number of slices that can fit in your chart - but too many slices will make the chart difficult to read. A maximum of 10 slices is recommended.
3. **[Slice/Data Label]** – a Pie/Doughnut chart must have % as a data label.

4. **[Legend]** – always display a Legend for a Pie Chart so the audience can correlate the individual slice data

Other Configurations Available Within Pie/Doughnut Charts:

5. **[Color by]** – default by "Dimension Value." This will affect how colors are arranged for each pie - you can choose between Single Color, Slice Order, or Dimension Value.
6. **[Manage Dimension value Color]** – to customize the slice color for Pie Dimension
7. **[Doughnut Size]** – the default is 0% for Pie charts and 50% for Doughnut charts. You can slide left and right to adjust the doughnut size.
8. **[Pie Slice Font Color, Size and Family]** – leave to the default black. This works across the color palette.
9. **[Slice Label]** – default is %. Other option includes None, Value (Raw Number) and Label (Dimension Labels).
10. **[Slice Label Text Contrast]** – leave to default unless you are making for a specific audience. Options include low, medium, and high.
11. **[Background Color, Border Radius and Opacity]** – customizable; please refer to page 8 for a detailed explanation.
12. **[Border Color, Weight, Style, and Shadow]** – customizable; please refer to page 8 for a detailed explanation.
13. **[Legend Position]** – default is right. Other options are left, bottom, top, and none.
14. **[Legend Alignment]** – default is middle. Other options are top and bottom
15. **[Legend Font Color, Size, and Family]** – theme default
16. **[Chart Header and Font Color]** – chart headers allow viewers to perform several actions on charts, such as data export, drilling up or down, and view charts in explorer tools. Please refer to page 12 for a detailed explanation.

I. Pie Chart

A Pie chart expresses a part-to-whole relationship in a data set. It will always add up to 100%. So, if, for instance, you want to show "How does 100% divide up into multiple shares?" you should always use a Pie/Doughnut Chart with % as a data label.

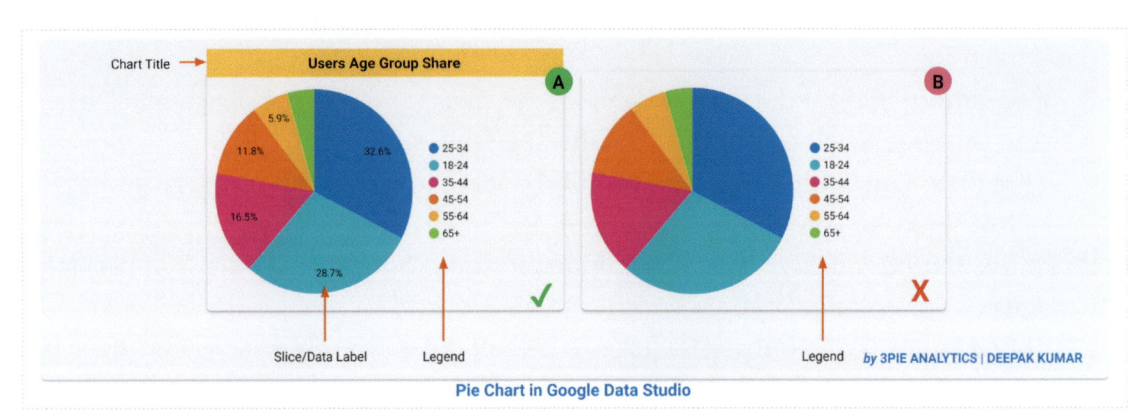

- In Chart B, we can quickly identify that the 25-34 group has the highest 'Users' share, but we can only guess the % share for any of age groups.
- Unlike a Scorecard, a Pie chart doesn't have a Metric name. In Chart B, we can't see which metric is used.

Chart Configurations:

1. **[Chart Title]** – add a chart title so audiences can see which metrics are used in the chart.
2. **[Pie Slices/Number of Slices]** – default is 10, the maximum number is 20. You should test for the number of slices that can fit in your chart - but too many slices will make the chart difficult to read. A maximum of 10 slices is recommended.
3. **[Slice/Data Label]** – a Pie chart must have % as a data label. Chart A in this example
4. **[Legend]** – always display a Legend for a Pie Chart so the audience can correlate the individual slice data
5. **[Background]** – this is gray in the above Scorecard, but the default will depend on how you have set up your theme.
6. **[Border Radius]** – 4 in this example
7. **[Border Color]** – this is transparent in the above Scorecard, but the default will depend on how you have set up your theme.
8. **[Border Shadow]** – applied in the above charts. The default is not selected

Page 28

Other Configurations: Left To Default

9. **[Color by]** – default by "Dimension Value."
10. **[Manage Dimension value Color]** – theme default
11. **[Doughnut Size]** – the default is 0% for a Pie Chart
12. **[Pie Slice Font Color, Size and Family]** – theme default
13. **[Slice/Data Label]** – default is %.
14. **[Slice Label Text Contrast]** – default, none
15. **[Background Opacity]** – default is 100%
16. **[Border Weight and Style]** – default, none. Please refer to page 8 for a detailed explanation.
17. **[Legend Font Color, Size and Family]** – theme default
18. **[Legend Alignment]** – default is right. Please refer to page 13 for a detailed explanation.
19. **[Chart Header and Font Color]** – chart headers allow viewers to perform several actions on charts, such as data export, drilling up or down, and view charts in explorer tools. Please refer to page 12 for a detailed explanation.

Recommended: Yes [A]

- Yes, this is one of the most widely used charts across the industry.
- If you want to show "how does 100% divide up into a few shares?", it's best practice to use only Pie/Doughnut Charts.

II. Doughnut Chart

A Doughnut chart expresses a part-to-whole relationship in a data set, and it will always add up to 100%. So, if, for instance, you want to show "how does 100% divide up into a few shares?" you should always use Pie/Doughnut Chart with % as a data label.

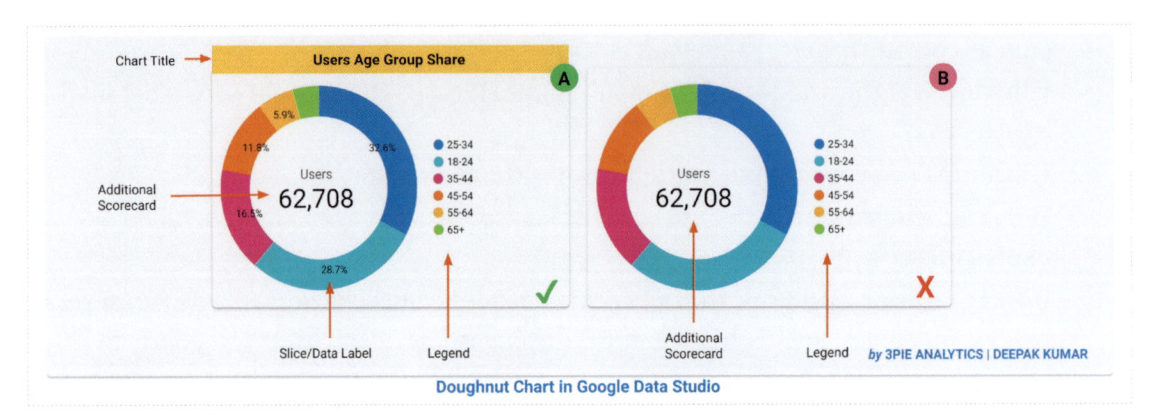

![Doughnut Chart in Google Data Studio]

- In Chart B, we can quickly identify that the 25-34 group has the highest 'Users' share, but we can only guess the % share for any of age groups.
- Unlike a Scorecard, a Doughnut chart doesn't have a Metric name. In Chart B, we can't see which metric is used.

Chart Configurations:

1. **[Chart Title]** – add a chart title so audiences can see which metrics are used in the chart.
2. **[Doughnut Size]** – 80% in this example and default is 50%
3. **[Extra Space in the Middle]** – doughnut Charts provide extra space in the middle and a scorecard has been used to display absolute value for the same metric.
4. **[Slice/Data Label]** – a Doughnut chart must have % as a data label. Chart A in this example
5. **[Legend]** – always display a Legend for a Doughnut Chart so the audience can correlate the individual slice data
6. **[Background]** – this is gray in the above Scorecard, but the default will depend on how you have set up your theme.
7. **[Border Radius]** – 4 in this example
8. **[Border Color]** – this is transparent in the above Scorecard, but the default will depend on how you have set up your theme.
9. **[Border Shadow]** – applied in the above charts. The default is not selected

Other Configurations: Left To Default

10. **[Color by]** – default by "Dimension Value."

Page 30

11. **[Manage Dimension value Color]** – theme default
12. **[Pie Slice Font Color, Size and Family]** – theme default
13. **[Slice/Data Label]** – default is %.
14. **[Slice Label Text Contrast]** – default, none
15. **[Background Opacity]** – default is 100%
16. **[Border Weight and Style]** – default, none. Please refer to page 8 for a detailed explanation.
17. **[Legend Font Color, Size and Family]** – theme default
18. **[Legend Alignment]** – default is right. Please refer to page 13 for a detailed explanation.
19. **[Chart Header and Font Color]** – chart headers allow viewers to perform several actions on charts, such as data export, drilling up or down, and view charts in explorer tools. Please refer to page 12 for a detailed explanation.

Recommended: Yes [A]

- Yes, this is one of the most widely used charts across the industry.
- If you want to show "how does 100% divide up into a few shares?", it's best practice to use only Pie/Doughnut Charts.
- My personal favorite, the advantage of using a doughnut chart has a space in the middle for a Scorecard. In this example, "The total users making up 100%". This way, audiences can compare against an individual element.

III. Pie/Doughnut Chart with Value as a Data Label

A Pie/Doughnut chart expresses a part-to-whole relationship in a data set, and it will always add up to 100%. So if, for instance, you want to show "how does 100% divide up into a few shares?" you should always use Pie/Doughnut Chart with % as a data label.

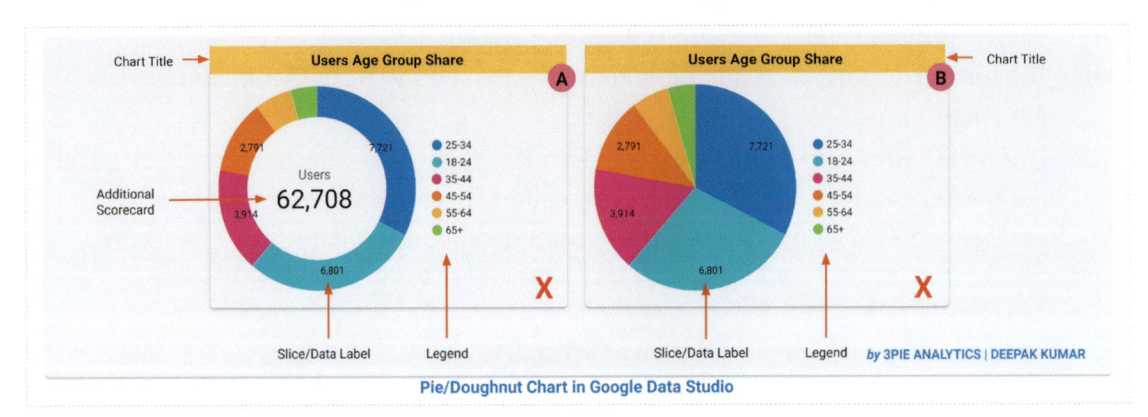

- In both Charts, we can see that the 25-34 group has the highest users, but we can only guess the % share for any age group. Your report audience will always expect more information from a Pie/Doughnut chart.

Chart Configurations:

1. **[Chart Title]** – add a chart title so audiences can see which metrics are used in the chart.
2. **[Doughnut Size]** – 80% in this example and default is 50%
3. **[Extra Space in the Middle]** – doughnut Charts provide extra space in the middle and a scorecard has been used to display absolute value for the same metric.
4. **[Slice/Data Label]** – number in this example and a Pie/Doughnut chart must have % as a data label.
5. **[Legend]** – always display a Legend for a Doughnut Chart so the audience can correlate the individual slice data
6. **[Background]** – this is gray in the above Scorecard, but the default will depend on how you have set up your theme.
7. **[Border Radius]** – 4 in this example
8. **[Border Color]** – this is transparent in the above Scorecard, but the default will depend on how you have set up your theme.
9. **[Border Shadow]** – applied in the above charts. The default is not selected

Other Configurations: Left To Default

10. **[Color by]** – default by "Dimension Value."
11. **[Manage Dimension value Color]** – theme default

Page 32

12. **[Pie Slice Font Color, Size and Family]** –theme default
13. **[Slice/Data Label]** – default is %.
14. **[Slice Label Text Contrast]** – default, none
15. **[Background Opacity]** – default is 100%
16. **[Border Weight and Style]** – default, none
17. **[Legend Font Color, Size and Family]** – theme default
18. **[Legend Alignment]** – default is right. Please refer to page 13 for a detailed explanation.
19. **[Chart Header and Font Color]** – please refer to page 12 for a detailed explanation.

Recommended: NO
- If you want to see a part-to-whole relationship in a data set, chart data labels should always be % and avoid having number labels at any cost.

IV. Column/Bar Chart as a Pie/Doughnut Chart Alternative

Column charts use vertical columns to compare different KPIs, while a Pie/Doughnut chart expresses a part-to-whole relationship in a data set. It is best practice to avoid Column/Bar charts as a Pie chart alternative.

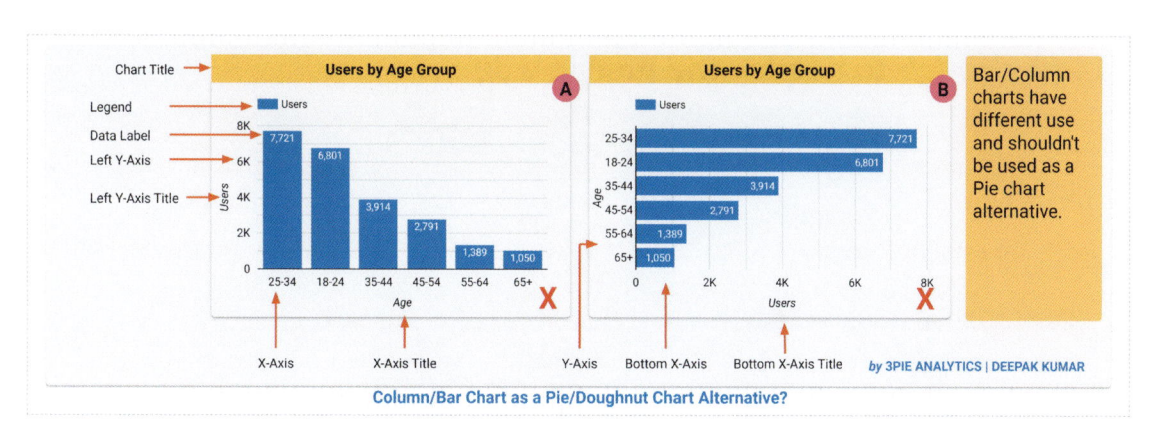

Column/Bar Chart as a Pie/Doughnut Chart Alternative?

- In both Charts, we can see that the 25-34 group has the highest users, but we can only guess the % share for any age group. Bar/Column charts have a different use case and should be avoided as an alternative to Pie/Doughnut charts.

Recommended: NO
- Bar/Column charts have different use and shouldn't be used as a Pie chart alternative.

Chapter 4: Bullet Charts

Bullet charts display a single metric performance and progress towards a certain goal or against a benchmark. You can optionally display a target value, and set up to 3 ranges.

Use case:

1. **Bullet Chart with Target and Ranges:** this is used to measure a single metric performance divided into three ranges and progress towards a goal or against target benchmarks.
2. **Bullet Chart without Target:** this can be configured to display the ranges for poor, average, and good. A maximum of 3 ranges is allowed.
3. **Bullet Chart with Target, Ranges, and Comparison:** to measure a metric performance divided into three ranges, progress towards a certain goal or against a benchmark and compare to the previous period

Recommended:

Yes, the default three ranges are set to 1,2,3 and target 1.5. You can set this according to your report objective and metric value. You can remove a range from the chart by setting it to 0. If you don't want ranges at all, set all 3 ranges to the same value (use a value large enough to display the metric value).

Bullet Chart in Google Data Studio		
Chart Type	Axis	Recommended
With Target and Ranges	Always	Yes (Personal Preference)
Without Target (Ranges Only)	Always	Yes
With Target, Ranges, and Comparison	Always	Yes

Recommended Configurations For Bullet Charts:

1. **[Bar Color and Range Color]** – default is blue for Metrics (Bar Color) and grey for Ranges. But you can customize based on your chart objective
2. **[Axis]** – always show Axis since it's not possible to display the data label.
3. **[Chart Title]** – bullet chart doesn't have a Legend Name. Best practice is to add a chart title so audiences can see which metrics are used in the chart

4. **[Default Range Limits and Target]** – default ranges limits are 1, 2, 3, and Target 1.5. These are set manually in the DATA tab, and the following range should be greater than the last one. A maximum of 3 ranges is allowed and you should adjust these to better fit your actual data. It's a best practice to use ranges and Targets for a Bullet Chart.
5. **[Data Label]** – unfortunately, it's not possible to display the Data Label in the Bullet chart. You can use a scorecard in the middle to show the metric value used in the Chart shown in the following example

Others Configurations Available Within Bullet Charts:

6. **[Axis Font Color, Size and Family]** – leave to the default black. This works across the color palette.
7. **[Axis Compact Number and Decimal Precision]** – default displayed as a Compact number with auto decimal precision
8. **[Background Color, Border Radius and Opacity]** – customizable; please refer to page 8 for a detailed explanation.
9. **[Border Color, Weight, Style, and Shadow]** – customizable; please refer to page 8 for a detailed explanation.
10. **[Chart Header and Font Color]** – chart headers allow viewers to perform several actions on charts, such as data export, drilling up or down, and view charts in explorer tools. Please refer to page 12 for a detailed explanation.

I. Bullet Chart: With Target and Ranges

This is used to measure a single metric performance divided into three ranges and progress towards a goal or against target benchmarks. Target value and ranges are optional.

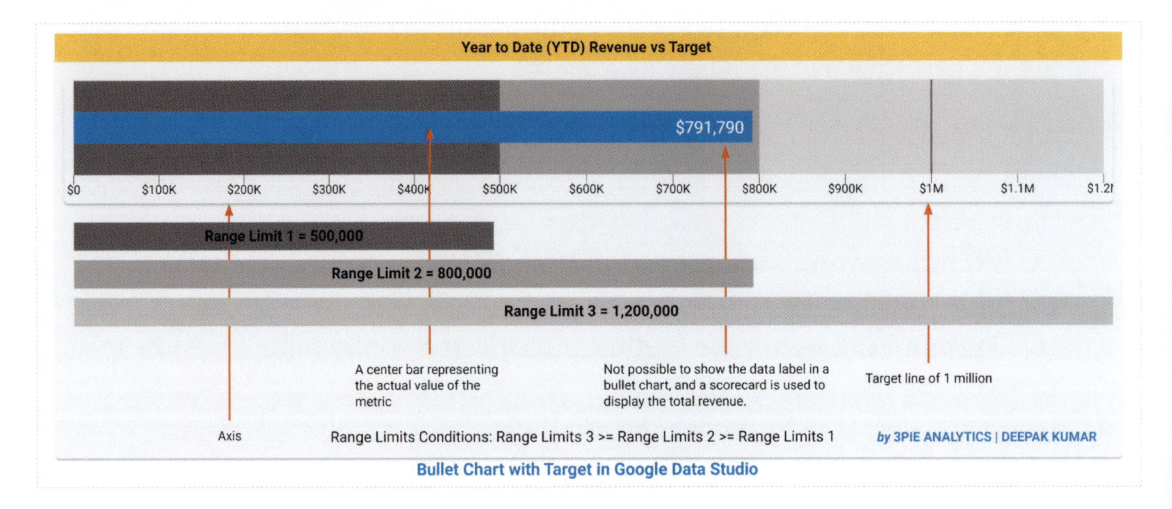

![Bullet Chart with Target in Google Data Studio showing Year to Date (YTD) Revenue vs Target with $791,790 actual value, Range Limit 1 = 500,000, Range Limit 2 = 800,000, Range Limit 3 = 1,200,000, and Target line of 1 million]

- A Gauge chart alternative in Google Data Studio. Bullet charts don't always need to be this big - this example is only used to explain details.
- A center blue bar shows the actual value of the metric. In this example that is 2021 YTD revenue.
- In this example, the target is set to 1 million and the blue line represents how far the target has reached so far against the Black target line
- **[Data Label - $791,790]** – unfortunately, it's not possible to display the Data Label in the Bullet chart. In the above example, a scorecard has been placed on top to show the exact revenue.

Chart Configurations:

1. **[Metrics]** – a center blue bar - color can be configured in the STYLE tab.
2. **[Chart Title]** – add a chart title so audiences can see the metrics used in the chart.
3. **[Data Label - $791,790]** – unfortunately, it's not possible to display the Data Label in the Bullet chart. In the above example, a scorecard has been placed on top to show the exact revenue.
4. **[Bar Color and Range Color]** – left to default this is blue for Bar Color and grey for Ranges.
5. **[Axis]** – always show Axis since it's not possible to display the data label.
6. **[Range Limits]** – these are set manually in the DATA tab, and the following range should be greater than the last one. A maximum of 3 ranges is allowed.

7. **[Target]** – target is also set manually, which is an optional metric. In this chart, target revenue is set as 1 million, and the blue line represents how far the target has reached so far.
8. **[Target Line and Color]** – show the target line based on the metric value. Color is Black by default and is not possible to change.
9. **[Background]** – this is gray in the above Scorecard, but the default will depend on how you have set up your theme.
10. **[Border Radius]** – 4 in this example
11. **[Border Color]** – this is transparent in the above Scorecard, but the default will depend on how you have set up your theme.
12. **[Border Shadow]** – applied in the above charts. The default is not selected

Other Configurations: Left To Default

13. **[Axis Font Color, Size and Family]** – theme default
14. **[Axis Compact Number and Decimal Precision]** – default as a Compact Numbers with Auto decimal precision
15. **[Background Opacity]** – default is 100%
16. **[Border Weight and Style]** – default, none
17. **[Chart Header and Font Color]** – chart headers allow viewers to perform several actions on charts, such as data export, drilling up or down, and view charts in explorer tools. Please refer to page 12 for a detailed explanation.

Recommended: Yes

- **Bullet charts with target and Ranges:** to display a single metric performance divided into three ranges and progress towards a goal or against target benchmarks.

II. Bullet Chart: Without Target (Ranges Only)

This is used to measure a metric performance divided into three ranges, compared to the previous period and progress towards a certain goal or against a benchmark.

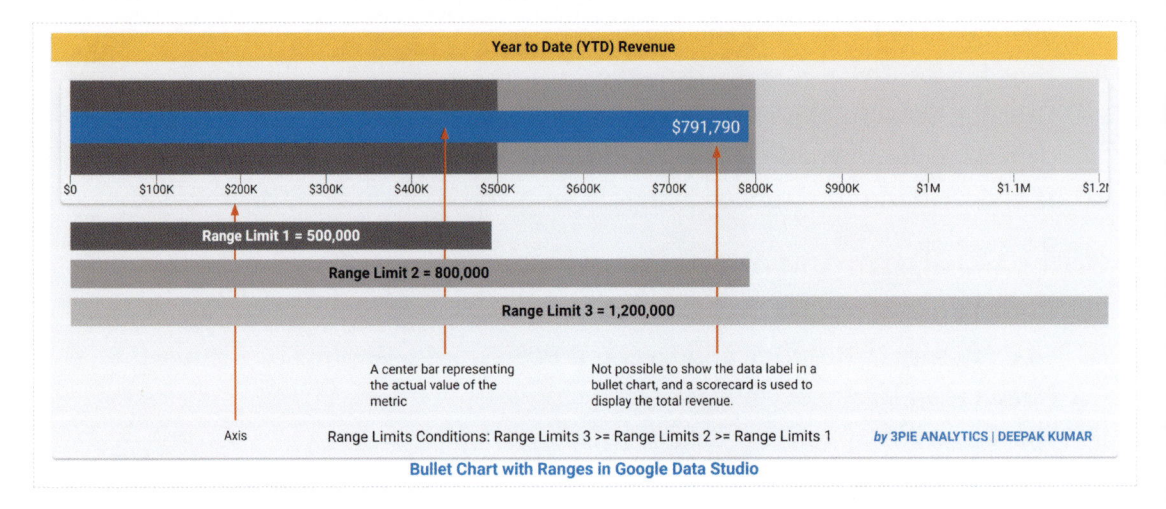

![Bullet Chart with Ranges in Google Data Studio showing Year to Date (YTD) Revenue of $791,790 with Range Limit 1 = 500,000, Range Limit 2 = 800,000, Range Limit 3 = 1,200,000. Range Limits Conditions: Range Limits 3 >= Range Limits 2 >= Range Limits 1. by 3PIE ANALYTICS | DEEPAK KUMAR]

– This is the same chart as above, only the target configuration has been removed.
– A Gauge chart alternative in Google Data Studio. Bullet charts don't always need to be this big - this example is only used to explain details.
– A center blue bar shows the actual value of the metric. In this example that is 2021 YTD revenue.
– **[Data Label - $791,790]** – Unfortunately, it's not possible to display the Data Label in the Bullet chart. In the above example, a scorecard has been placed on top to show the exact revenue.
– In this example, we have not set a target value. It can be considered the revenue ranges up to 500k as poor, above 500k and up to 800k as an average, and above 800k as good.

Chart Configurations:

1. **[Metrics]** – a center blue bar - color can be configured in the STYLE tab.
2. **[Chart Title]** – add a chart title so audiences can see the metrics used in the chart.
3. **[Data Label - $791,790]** – unfortunately, it's not possible to display the Data Label in the Bullet chart. In the above example, a scorecard has been placed on top to show the exact revenue.
4. **[Bar Color and Range Color]** – left to default this is blue for Bar Color and grey for Ranges.
5. **[Axis]** – always show Axis since it's not possible to display the data label.
6. **[Range Limits]** – these are set manually in the DATA tab, and the following range should be greater than the last one. A maximum of 3 ranges is allowed.

7. **[Target Line and Color]** – show the target line based on the metric value. Color is Black by default and is not possible to change.
8. **[Background]** – this is gray in the above Scorecard, but the default will depend on how you have set up your theme.
9. **[Border Radius]** – 4 in this example
10. **[Border Color]** – this is transparent in the above Scorecard, but the default will depend on how you have set up your theme.
11. **[Border Shadow]** – applied in the above charts. The default is not selected

Other Configurations: Left To Default

12. **[Target]** – none, set manually in the DATA tab
13. **[Axis Font Color, Size and Family]** – theme default
14. **[Axis Compact Number and Decimal Precision]** – default as a Compact Numbers with Auto decimal precision
15. **[Background Opacity]** – default is 100%
16. **[Border Weight and Style]** – default, none
17. **[Chart Header and Font Color]** – chart headers allow viewers to perform several actions on charts, such as data export, drilling up or down, and view charts in explorer tools. Please refer to page 12 for a detailed explanation.

Recommended: Yes

- **Bullet charts with ranges (without target):** to measure a metric performance divided into 3 ranges, for example, ranges for poor, average, and good.

III. Bullet Chart: With Target Ranges and Comparison

This is used to measure a metric performance divided into three ranges, progress towards a certain goal or against a benchmark and compare to the previous period.

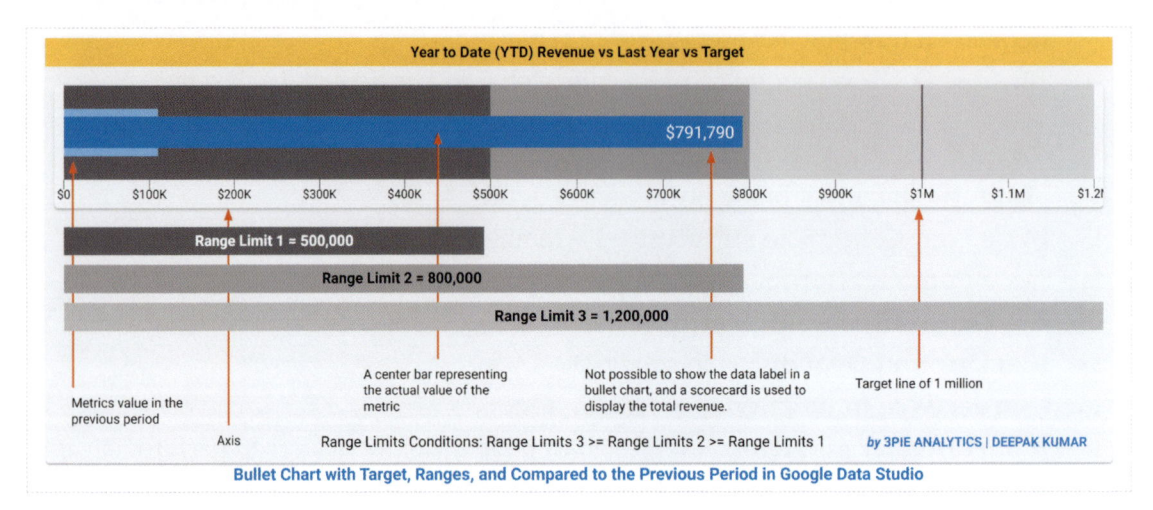

Bullet Chart with Target, Ranges, and Compared to the Previous Period in Google Data Studio

- A Gauge chart alternative in Google Data Studio. Bullet charts don't always need to be this big - this example is only used to explain details.
- A center blue bar shows the actual value of the metric. In this example that is 2021 YTD revenue.
- **[Data Label - $791,790]** – Unfortunately, it's not possible to display the Data Label in the Bullet chart. In the above example, a scorecard has been placed on top to show the exact revenue.
- In this example, target revenue is set as 1 million, with the blue line representing how far the target has reached so far. Light blue displays the revenue of the last year during the same period.

Chart Configurations:

1. **[Metrics]** – a center blue bar - color can be configured in the STYLE tab.
2. **[Chart Title]** – add a chart title so audiences can see the metrics used in the chart.
3. **[Comparison]** – optional, in the above chart, from the previous period
4. **[Data Label - $791,790]** – unfortunately, it's not possible to display the Data Label in the Bullet chart. In the above example, a scorecard has been placed on top to show the exact revenue.
5. **[Bar Color and Range Color]** – left to default this is blue for Bar Color and grey for Ranges.
6. **[Bar Color - Previous Period]** – this will be the light color of the selected Bar color; light blue in this example displays the last year's revenue during the same period.

7. **[Axis]** – always show Axis since it's not possible to display the data label.
8. **[Range Limits]** – these are set manually in the DATA tab, and the following range should be greater than the last one. A maximum of 3 ranges is allowed.
9. **[Target]** – Target is also set manually, which is an optional metric. In this chart, target revenue is set as 1 million, and the blue line represents how far the target has reached so far.
10. **[Target Line and Color]** – Show the target line based on the metric value. Color is Black by default and is not possible to change.
11. **[Background]** – this is gray in the above Scorecard, but the default will depend on how you have set up your theme.
12. **[Border Radius]** – 4 in this example
13. **[Border Color]** – this is transparent in the above Scorecard, but the default will depend on how you have set up your theme.
14. **[Border Shadow]** – applied in the above charts. The default is not selected

Other Configurations: Left To Default

15. **[Axis Font Color, Size and Family]** – theme default
16. **[Axis Compact Number and Decimal Precision]** – default as a Compact Numbers with Auto decimal precision
17. **[Background Opacity]** – default is 100%
18. **[Border Weight and Style]** – default, none. Please refer to page 8 for a detailed explanation.
19. **[Chart Header and Font Color]** – chart headers allow viewers to perform several actions on charts, such as data export, drilling up or down, and view charts in explorer tools. Please refer to page 12 for a detailed explanation.

Recommended: Yes

- **Bullet chart with target and compared to the previous period:** to measure a metric performance divided into three ranges, compared to the previous period and progress towards a certain goal or against a benchmark.

Chapter 5: Gauge Charts

Gauge charts display a single metric performance and progress towards a certain goal or against a benchmark.

Use case:

1. **Gauge Chart With Target Only:** this is used to measure a metric performance and progress towards a certain goal or against a benchmark.
2. **Gauge Chart With Ranges Only (Without Target):** this can be configured to display the ranges for poor, average, good, very good, and excellent. Maximum 5 ranges are allowed
3. **Gauge Chart With Target and Comparison:** this is used to measure a metric performance and compare to the Previous period; progress towards a certain goal/benchmark, and assign up to 5 ranges
4. **Gauge Chart With Target, Ranges, and Comparison:** All above

Recommended:

Yes, but a default Gauge Chart doesn't provide any meaningful information without a Target or Ranges. Therefore, it's best practice to set a target or ranges.

Gauge Chart in Google Data Studio		
Chart Type	Axis	Recommended
Default Gauge Chart	N/A	No
With Target Only	Always	Yes (Personal Preference)
With Ranges Only (Without Target)	Always	Yes
With Target and Comparison	Always	No
With Target, Ranges, and Comparison	Always	No

Recommended Configurations For Bullet Charts:

1. **[Chart Title]** – title is not absolutely necessary. Still, personally, I always prefer to have a title for each chart.
2. **[Comparison]** – if your data set allows, you should always display the comparison.
3. **[Bar Color]** – default is blue for Metrics (Bar Color) and grey for Ranges. But you can customize based on your reporting template

4. **[Range Color]** – configurable in the STYLE tab. The maximum value will have the lightest Color.
5. **[Range Limits]** – default is none and doesn't provide any meaningful information without a Target or Ranges. Therefore, it's best practice to set a target or range. Up to 5 ranges can be set and are configurable in the STYLE tab.
6. **[Axis]** – always show axis so users can see the min and max value set.
7. **[Axis Min and Max Value]** – default is auto, and you should set this based on the reporting objective and the Metric value
8. **[Target]** – default is none, set manually in the STYLE tab.
9. **[Target Line Color and Color]** – show the target line based on the target value. Default Color is set too Black, and it is not possible to change it.
10. **[Metrics Name and Value]** – selected metric for the chart displayed in the middle looks like a Scorecard with a compact number configuration. By default displayed and It can be hidden by selecting **"Hide Metric Name"** and **"Hide Metric Value"**, but you should always display the metric name so the report audience can identify the metrics used in the chart.

Others Configurations Available Within Bullet Charts:

11. **[Metrics Compact Number and Decimal Precision]** – default displayed as a Compact number with auto decimal precision
12. **[Missing Data]** – at default, this will show as "No data". Other options include: 0, - ("-"), null, and Blank (""). Please refer to page 9 for a detailed explanation
13. **[Labels Font Color, Size and Family]** – leave to the default black. This works across the color palette.
14. **[Background Color, Border Radius and Opacity]** – customizable; please refer to page 8 for a detailed explanation.
15. **[Border Color, Weight, Style, and Shadow]** – customizable; please refer to page 8 for a detailed explanation.
16. **[Chart Header and Font Color]** – chart headers allow viewers to perform several actions on charts, such as data export, drilling up or down, and view charts in explorer tools. Please refer to page 12 for a detailed explanation.

I. Default Gauge Chart

Gauge charts display a single metric performance. Axis Min and Max values are automatically defined. By default, Gauge Chart doesn't provide any meaningful information.

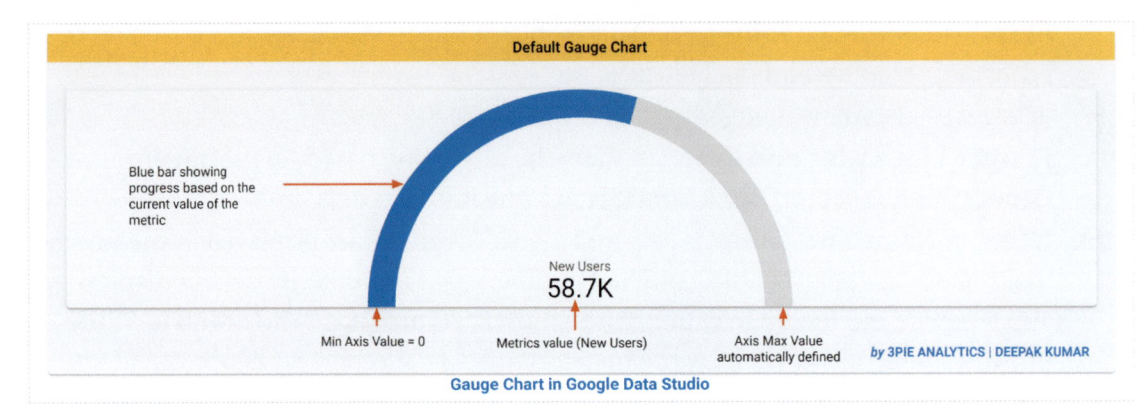

Default Gauge Chart

Blue bar showing progress based on the current value of the metric

New Users
58.7K

Min Axis Value = 0   Metrics value (New Users)   Axis Max Value automatically defined   *by 3PIE ANALYTICS | DEEPAK KUMAR*

Gauge Chart in Google Data Studio

- By default, a Gauge chart doesn't have Target and Range configurations.
- Metrics numbers are displayed as a compact number.
- Minimum and maximum axis values are automatically defined.

Chart Configurations:

1. **[Chart Title]** – the title is not absolutely necessary for a Gauge Chart. Still, personally, I always prefer to have a title for each chart.
2. **[Metrics]** – the selected metric for the chart displayed in the middle looks like a Scorecard with a compact number configuration. It can be hidden by selecting **"Hide Metric Name"** and **"Hide Metric Value"**.
3. **[Background]** – this is gray in the above Scorecard, but the default will depend on how you have set up your theme.
4. **[Border Radius]** – 4 in this example
5. **[Border Color]** – this is transparent in the above Scorecard, but the default will depend on how you have set up your theme.
6. **[Border Shadow]** – applied in the above charts. The default is not selected

Other Configurations: Left To Default

7. **[Comparison]** – none, set manually in the DATA tab.
8. **[Bar Color]** – default, blue
9. **[Range Color]** – default, grey
10. **[Range Limits]** – none
11. **[Axis]** – default, unchecked
12. **[Axis Min and Max Value]** – available if you have selected Axis configuration
13. **[Target]** – default, not set

14. **[Missing Data]** – default "No data." Please refer to page 9 for a detailed explanation.
15. **[Label Font Color, Size and Family]** – theme default
16. **[Metrics Name and Value]** – default, selected
17. **[Background Opacity]** – default is 100%
18. **[Border Weight and Style]** – default, none. Please refer to the page 8 for a detailed explanation.
19. **[Chart Header and Font Color]** – chart headers allow viewers to perform several actions on charts, such as data export, drilling up or down, and view charts in explorer tools. Please refer to page 12 for a detailed explanation.

Recommended: No

- By default, a Gauge Chart doesn't provide any meaningful information without a Target or Ranges.

II. Gauge Chart With Target Only

This is used to measure a metric performance and progress towards a certain goal or against a benchmark.

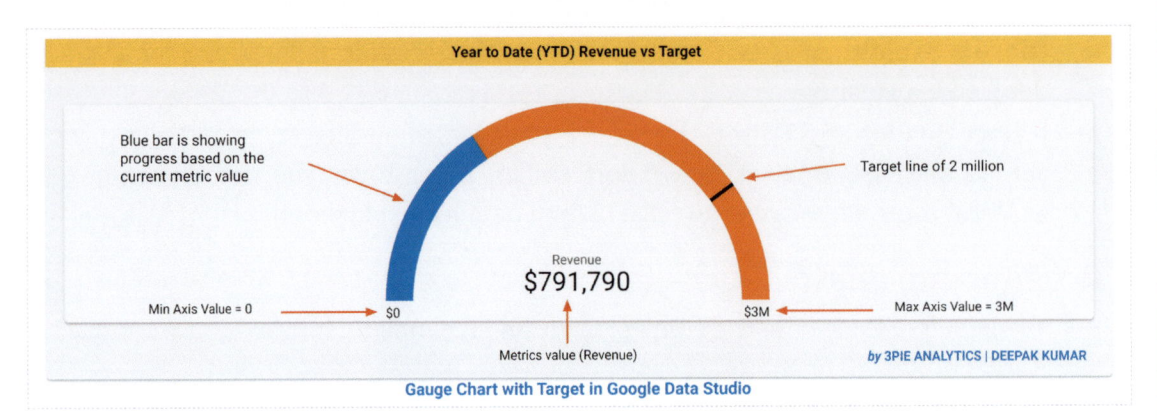

Year to Date (YTD) Revenue vs Target

Blue bar is showing progress based on the current metric value

Target line of 2 million

Revenue
$791,790

Min Axis Value = 0 $0 $3M   Max Axis Value = 3M

Metrics value (Revenue)

by 3PIE ANALYTICS | DEEPAK KUMAR

Gauge Chart with Target in Google Data Studio

- A Bullet chart alternative in Google Data Studio. A Gauge chart doesn't need to be this big - this example is only used to explain details.
- A center blue bar represents the actual value of the Metric, in this example, 2021 YTD revenue. Metrics value is shown in the middle, looking like a Scorecard.
- In this example, target revenue is set at 2 million, with the blue line representing how far the target has reached so far.

Chart Configurations:

1. **[Chart Title]** – title is not absolutely necessary for a Gauge Chart. Still, personally, I always prefer to have a title for each chart.
2. **[Metrics]** – selected metric for the chart displayed in the middle looks like a Scorecard with a compact number configuration. It can be hidden by selecting **"Hide Metric Name"** and **"Hide Metric Value"**.
3. **[Metric Compact Number and Decimal Precision]** – default as a Compact Numbers and deselected in this example with decimal precision change to 0 from Auto
4. **[Bar Color]** – left to default is blue for Metrics (Bar Color).
5. **[Axis]** – always show axis so users can see the min and max value set.
6. **[Axis Min and Max Value]** – min value set to 0 and max to 3M. You should set this based on the reporting objective and the Metric value
7. **[Target]** – 2 million, set manually in the STYLE tab.
8. **[Target Line and Color]** – show the target line based on the metric value. Color is Black by default and is not possible to change.
9. **[Range Color]** – changed to chrome yellow from default grey
10. **[Background]** – this is gray in the above Scorecard, but the default will depend on how you have set up your theme.

11. **[Border Radius]** – 4 in this example
12. **[Border Color]** – this is transparent in this Scorecard, but the default will depend on how you have set up your theme.
13. **[Border Shadow]** – applied in the above charts. The default is not selected

Other Configurations: Left To Default

14. **[Comparison]** –none, set manually in the DATA tab.
15. **[Range Limits]** – none
16. **[Missing Data]** – default, "No data". Please refer to the page 9 for a detailed explanation.
17. **[Font Color, Size and Family]** – theme default
18. **[Metrics Name and Value]** – default, selected
19. **[Background Opacity]** – default is 100%
20. **[Border Weight and Style]** – default, none. Please refer to the page 8 for a detailed explanation.
21. **[Chart Header and Font Color]** – chart headers allow viewers to perform several actions on charts, such as data export, drilling up or down, and view charts in explorer tools. Please refer to page 12 for a detailed explanation.

Recommended: Yes

- **Gauge Chart With Target Only:** this is used to measure a metric performance and progress towards a certain goal or against a benchmark.

III. Gauge Chart With Ranges Only (Without Target)

With Ranges, It can be configured to display the ranges for poor, average, good, very good, and excellent. A maximum of 5 ranges are allowed.

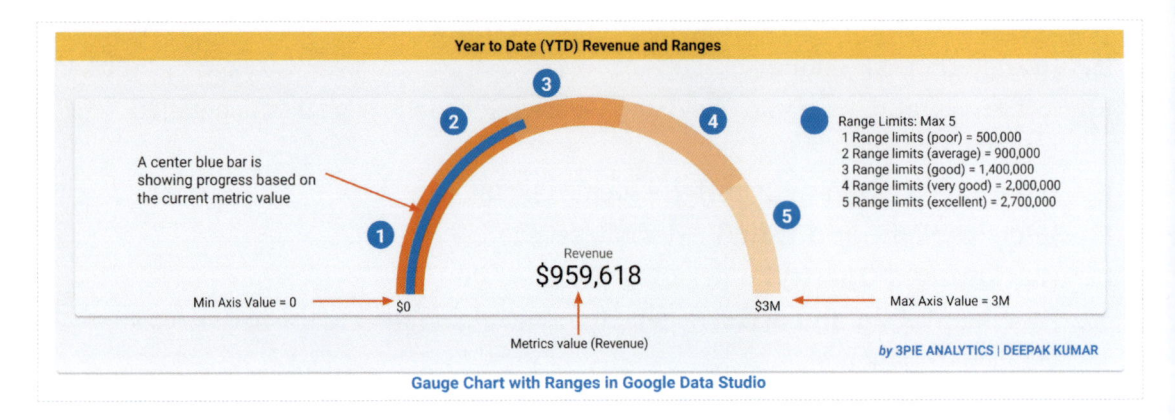

Gauge Chart with Ranges in Google Data Studio

- A Bullet chart alternative in Google Data Studio. A Gauge chart doesn't need to be this big - this example is only used to explain details.
- A center blue bar represents the actual value of the Metric, in this example, 2021 YTD revenue. Metrics value is shown in the middle, looking like a Scorecard.
- In this example, a Gauge Chart is used to display the ranges for poor, average, good, very good, and excellent. You can also have three ranges like Bullet Chart, and a maximum of five ranges can be set in a Gauge Chart.

Chart Configurations:

1. **[Chart Title]** – title is not absolutely necessary for a Gauge Chart. Still, personally, I always prefer to have a title for each chart.
2. **[Metrics]** – selected metric for the chart displayed in the middle looks like a Scorecard with a compact number configuration. It can be hidden by selecting **"Hide Metric Name" and "Hide Metric Value".**
3. **[Metric Compact Number and Decimal Precision]** – default as a Compact Numbers and deselected in this example with decimal precision change to 0 from Auto
4. **[Bar Color]** – left to default is blue for Metrics (Bar Color).
5. **[Range Color]** – set to Chrome Yellow and configurable in the STYLE tab. The maximum value will have the lightest color.
6. **[Range Limits]** – a maximum of 5 ranges. In this example, revenue ranges up to 500k as poor, above 500k and up to 900k as average, above 500k and up to 900k as good, above 500k and up to 900k as very good, and above 500k and up to 900k as excellent
7. **[Axis]** – always show axis so users can see the min and max value set.

8. **[Axis Min and Max Value]** – min value set to 0 and max to 3M. You should set this based on the reporting objective and the Metric value
9. **[Target]** – 2 million, set manually in the STYLE tab.
10. **[Target Line and Color]** – show the target line based on the metric value. Color is Black by default and is not possible to change.
11. **[Range Color]** – changed to chrome yellow from default grey
12. **[Background]** – this is gray in the above Scorecard, but the default will depend on how you have set up your theme.
13. **[Border Radius]** – 4 in this example
14. **[Border Color]** – this is transparent in this Scorecard, but the default will depend on how you have set up your theme.
15. **[Border Shadow]** – applied in the above charts. The default is not selected

Other Configurations: Left To Default

16. **[Comparison]** –none, set manually in the DATA tab.
17. **[Missing Data]** – default "No data." Please refer to page 9 for a detailed explanation.
18. **[Font Color, Size and Family]** – theme default
19. **[Metrics Name and Value]** – default, selected
20. **[Background Opacity]** – default is 100%
21. **[Border Weight and Style]** – default, none. Please refer to the page 8 for a detailed explanation.
22. **[Chart Header and Font Color]** – chart headers allow viewers to perform several actions on charts, such as data export, drilling up or down, and view charts in explorer tools. Please refer to page 12 for a detailed explanation.

Recommended: Yes

- **Gauge Chart With Ranges Only (Without Target):** With Ranges, It can be configured to display the ranges for poor, average, good, very good, and excellent. A maximum of 5 ranges are allowed.

IV. Gauge Chart With Target and Comparison

This is used to measure a metric performance divided into five ranges, progress towards a certain goal or against a benchmark and compare to the previous period.

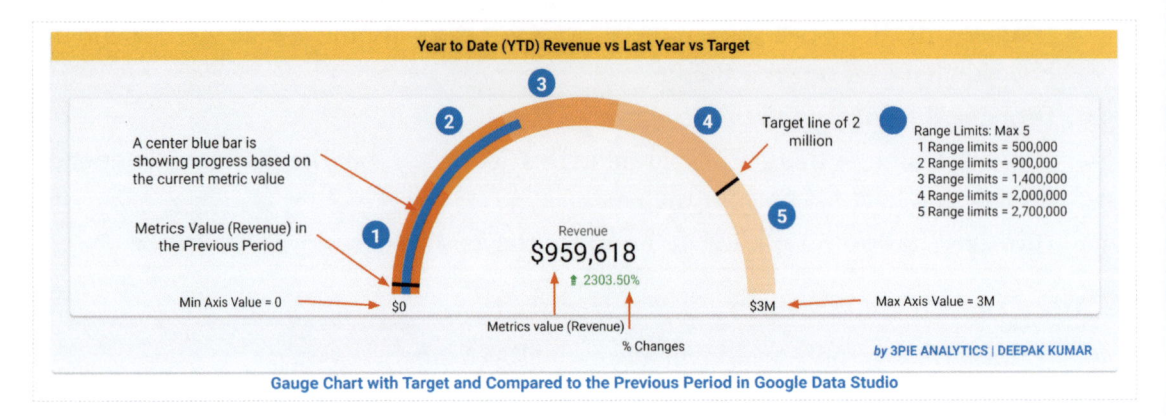

Gauge Chart with Target and Compared to the Previous Period in Google Data Studio

- A Bullet chart alternative in Google Data Studio. A Gauge chart doesn't need to be this big - this example is only used to explain details.
- A center blue bar represents the actual value of the Metric, in this example, 2021 YTD revenue. Metrics value is shown in the middle, looking like a Scorecard.
- In this example, target revenue is set at 2 million, with the blue line representing how far the target has reached so far. The left black line is showing the revenue of the last year during the same period.

Chart Configurations:

1. **[Chart Title]** – title is not absolutely necessary for a Gauge Chart. Still, personally, I always prefer to have a title for each chart.
2. **[Metrics]** – selected metric for the chart displayed in the middle looks like a Scorecard with a compact number configuration. It can be hidden by selecting **"Hide Metric Name"** and **"Hide Metric Value".**
3. **[Comparison]** – optional, in the above chart, from the previous period
4. **[Metric Compact Number and Decimal Precision]** – default as a Compact Numbers and deselected in this example with decimal precision change to 0 from Auto
5. **[Bar Color]** – left to default is blue for Metrics (Bar Color).
6. **[Range Color]** – Set to Chrome Yellow and configurable in the STYLE tab. The maximum value will have the lightest color.
7. **[Range Limits]** – A maximum of 5 ranges. In this example, revenue ranges up to 500k as poor, above 500k and up to 900k as average, above 500k and up to 900k as good, above 500k and up to 900k as very good, and above 500k and up to 900k as excellent

8. **[Axis]** – always show axis so users can see the min and max value set.
9. **[Axis Min and Max Value]** – min value set to 0 and max to 3M. You should set this based on the reporting objective and the Metric value
10. **[Target]** – 2 million, set manually in the STYLE tab.
11. **[Target Line and Color]** – show the target line based on the metric value. Color is Black by default and is not possible to change.
12. **[Range Color]** – changed to chrome yellow from default grey
13. **[Background]** – this is gray in the above Scorecard, but the default will depend on how you have set up your theme.
14. **[Border Radius]** – 4 in this example
15. **[Border Color]** – this is transparent in this Scorecard, but the default will depend on how you have set up your theme.
16. **[Border Shadow]** – applied in the above charts. The default is not selected

Other Configurations: Left To Default

17. **[Comparison Metric Color]** – default **green for the increase** and **red for a decrease,**
18. **[Comparison Metric - Compact Number]** – default unselected
19. **[Comparison Metric - Decimal Precision]** – default auto
20. **[Comparison Metric - Show Absolute Change]** – default unselected
21. **[Missing Data]** – default "No data." Please refer to page 9 for a detailed explanation.
22. **[Font Color, Size and Family]** – theme default
23. **[Metrics Name and Value]** – default, selected
24. **[Background Opacity]** – default is 100%
25. **[Border Weight and Style]** – default, none. Please refer to the page 8 for a detailed explanation.
26. **[Chart Header and Font Color]** – chart headers allow viewers to perform several actions on charts, such as data export, drilling up or down, and view charts in explorer tools. Please refer to page 12 for a detailed explanation.

Recommended: Yes

- **Gauge Chart With Target and Comparison:** to measure a metric performance divided into five ranges, progress towards a certain goal or against a benchmark and compare to the previous period.

Chapter 6: Line Charts/Time Series Charts

A line chart shows trends over time and works similarly to Area Chart except the inside area is not plotted. There are three types of line charts available and all are similar in functionality just displayed differently. X-Axis must be a date value for Line Charts.

Use case:

1. **Line Chart – Single Axis:** to trend over time.
2. **Line Chart – Double-Axis:** to trend over time but if one of the selected metrics is significantly smaller than the rest. Best practice to put those metrics on the second's Axis. Else line may a straight line on the X-Axis.
3. **Sparkline:** by default, everything is unselected except the line representing the data. Most cases used just below a Scorecard later shown

Recommended:

Yes, it is one of the most widely used charts across the industry.

Gauge Chart in Google Data Studio		
Chart Type	Axis	Recommended
Line Chart — Single Axis	Always	Yes
Line Chart — Two Axis	Always	Yes
Sparkline	n/a	Yes

Recommended Configurations For Line Charts:

1. **[Chart Title]** – in a Line chart, you have the option to display both Axis together with Legend, and the title is not necessary, but personally, I always prefer to have a title for each chart.
2. **[Data Label]** – not a common practice to display data labels in Line Charts and best to avoid.
3. **[Series/Line Color]** – individually customizable
4. **[Breakdown Dimension]** – only available if you have a single metric configuration. Breakdown Dimension, selected in the DATA tab.
5. **[X and Y-Axis]** – X-Axis must be date value therefore its not necessary to display X-Axis, but its best practice to display at least Y-Axis.
6. **[X and Y-Axis Title]** – only if you have two Axis configuration
7. **[Axis Min and Max Value]** – leave this to default auto and will adjust the bar height automatically based on the metric value.

8. **[Reference Line]** – add average reference lines to quickly identify the above average value
9. **[Legend]** – for a single axis column, chart legend is not necessary, but if your chart has more than one metric or breakdown dimension, always display Legend.

Others Configurations Available Within Line Charts:

10. **[Chart Type Selector]** – each series can be selected to display as the Line or Bar Chart, either on Left or Right Axis
11. **[Commutative]** – by default it's unselected and configured individually for each series
12. **[Show point and Data Label]** – individually customizable for each series
13. **[Compact Number and Decimal Precision]** – Compact Numbers and decimal precision are visible if you have selected "Show Data Labels"
14. **[Trendline]** – default unselected and options are Linear, Exponential, and Polynomial. They are configured individually for each series.
15. **[Reference Line]** – please refer to page 14 for a detailed explanation.
16. **[Missing Data]** – three options include "Line to zero" (Default Option), "Line breaks", and "Linear Interpolation". Please refer to page 9 for a detailed explanation.
17. **[Line Smoothness]** – default unselected
18. **[Reverse X and Y-Axis]** – individually or both Axis can be reversed.
19. **[Log Scale]** – log scales are automatically defined based on the Metrics value and will affect both Left Y-Axis and Line Position.
20. **[Grid Configuration]** – consists of Axis Color, Grid Color, Font Family, Font Size, Label Font Size, and Inner Chart Backboard & Border color.
21. **[Axis Font Color, Size and Family]** – leave to the default black. This works across the color palette.
22. **[Background Color, Border Radius, and Opacity]** – customizable; please refer to page 8 for a detailed explanation.
23. **[Border Color, Weight, and Style]** – customizable; please refer to page 8 for a detailed explanation.
24. **[Legend]** – the default position is top left. Other options are left, bottom, top, and none. Please refer to page 13 for a detailed explanation.
25. **[Chart Header and Font Color]** – chart headers allow viewers to perform several actions on charts, such as data export, drilling up or down, and view charts in explorer tools. Please refer to page 12 for a detailed explanation.

I. Line Chart: Double Axis

Line charts are best for tracking changes over short or long overtime. Compare how several things change over time relative to each other. When minor changes exist, line graphs are better than bar graphs. So If you hear that key phrase "over time," that's your clue to consider using line charts for your data.

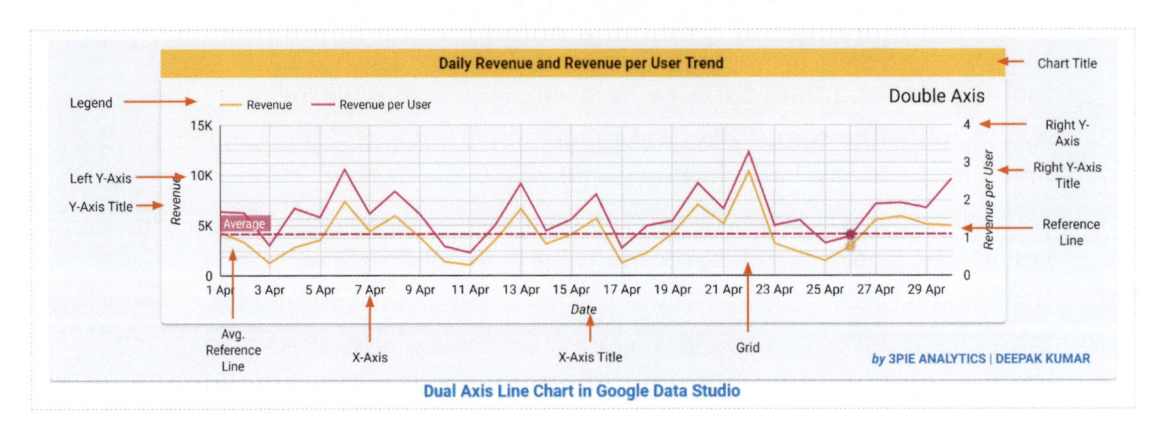

Dual Axis Line Chart in Google Data Studio

- In this chart, we display the daily Revenue and Revenue per User trend
- **[X and Y-Axis]** – X-Axis must be a date value
- **[Dual Axis]** – revenue on the left Y-Axis and Revenue per user on right Y-Axis

Chart Configurations:

1. **[Chart Title]** – in a Line chart, you have the option to display both Axis together with Legend, and the title is not necessary, but personally, I always prefer to have a title for each chart.
2. **[Data Label]** – not a common practice to display data labels in Line Charts and best to avoid.
3. **[Series/Line Color]** – theme default and individually customizable
4. **[Breakdown Dimension]** – only available if you have a single metric configuration. Breakdown Dimension, selected in the DATA tab.
5. **[X and Y-Axis]** – X-Axis must be date value therefore its not necessary to display X-Axis, but its best practice to display at least Y-Axis.
6. **[X and Y-Axis Title]** – only if you have two Axis configuration
7. **[Reference Line]** – average in this example, max ten reference lines are allowed.
8. **[Legend]** – always display legend if your chart has more than one metric or breakdown dimension.

Other Configurations: Left To Default

9. **[Chart Type Selector]** – each series can be selected to display as the Line or Bar

10. **[Show Cumulative]** – As a cumulative number
11. **[Show Points]** – Add a point on each data point
12. **[Show Data Labels]** – show number at each data point
13. **[Number Format]** – Compact Numbers and decimal precision. Visible if you have selected "Show Data Labels"
14. **[Series/line Color]** – you can assign unique Color for each series
15. **[Reference Line]** – Please refer to page 13 for a detailed explanation.
16. **[Missing Data]** – three options including Line to zero (Default Option), Line breaks, and Linear Interpolation. Please refer to page 9 for a detailed explanation.
17. **[Line Smoothness]** – default unselected
18. **[Axis Min and Max Value]** – leave to default or area plotted at some point might go above the Axis.
19. **[Custom Interval for Both Axis]** – leave to default Auto. Interval controls the Axis value displayed on both Axis. 7 Interval on X-Axis will have 4 data points for a month and 12 for a year.
20. **[Log Scale]** – Log scales are automatically defined based on the Metrics value and will change both Left Y-Axis and Line position
21. **[Grid Configuration]** – leave this to default. This will automatically adapt the configurations based on your chart size and color. Consists of Axis Color, Grid Color, Font Family, Font Size, Label Font Size, Chart Backboard, and Border color:
22. **[Background and Border]** – customizable; Please refer to page 8 for a detailed explanation.
23. **[Legend]** – the default position is top. Other options are left, bottom, top, and none. Legend alignment (left, centre, right), Legend color, Font Family, Font Size, and Max Lines are also customizable. Please refer to page 13 for a detailed explanation.
24. **[Chart Header]** – chart headers allow viewers to perform several actions on charts, such as data export, drilling up or down, and view charts in explorer tools. Please refer to page 12 for a detailed explanation.

Recommended: Yes, See The Chart Version That Suits Your Need

- **Line Chart – Double-Axis:** to trend over time but if one of the data set compared is significantly smaller than the rest. Best practice to put those metrics on the second's Axis. Else line may a straight line on the X-Axis.
- **Line Chart – Single Axis:** to trend over time.
- **Sparkline:** by default, everything is unselected except the line representing the data. Most cases used just below a Scorecard later shown

II. Line Chart: Single Axis

Line charts are best for tracking changes over short or long overtime. Compare how several things change over time relative to each other. When minor changes exist, line graphs are better than bar graphs. So If you hear that key phrase "over time," that's your clue to consider using line charts for your data.

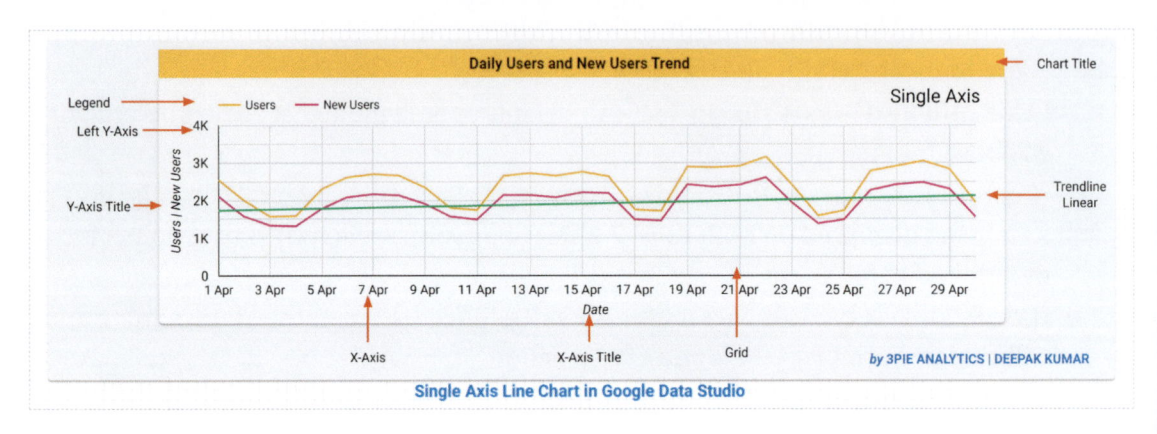

Single Axis Line Chart in Google Data Studio

- In this chart, we display the Daily Users and New Users Trend with Linear Trendline
- **[X and Y-Axis]** – X-Axis must be a date value
- **[Single Axis]** – both metrics displayed on the left Y-Axis

Chart Configurations:

1. **[Chart Title]** – in a Line chart, you have the option to display both Axis together with Legend, and the title is not necessary, but personally, I always prefer to have a title for each chart.
2. **[Data Label]** – not a common practice to display data labels in Line Charts and best to avoid.
3. **[Series/Line Color]** – theme default and individually customizable
4. **[Breakdown Dimension]** – only available if you have a single metric configuration. Breakdown Dimension, selected in the DATA tab.
5. **[X and Y-Axis]** – X-Axis must be date value therefore its not necessary to display X-Axis, but its best practice to display at least Y-Axis.
6. **[X and Y-Axis Title]** – only if you have two Axis configuration
7. **[Reference Line]** – average in this example, max ten reference lines are allowed.
8. **[Legend]** – for a single axis column, chart legend is not necessary, but if your chart has more than one metric or breakdown dimension, always display Legend.

Other Configurations: Left To Default

9. **[Chart Type Selector]** – each series can be selected to display as the Line or Bar
10. **[Show Cumulative]** – as a cumulative number
11. **[Show Points]** – add a point on each data point
12. **[Show Data Labels]** – show number at each data point
13. **[Number Format]** – Compact Numbers and decimal precision. Visible if you have selected "Show Data Labels"
14. **[Series/line Color]** – you can assign unique Color for each series
15. **[Reference Line]** – Ppease refer to page 13 for a detailed explanation.
16. **[Missing Data]** – three options including Line to zero (Default Option), Line breaks, and Linear Interpolation. Please refer to page 9 for a detailed explanation.
17. **[Line Smoothness]** – default unselected
18. **[Axis Min and Max Value]** – leave to default or area plotted at some point might go above the Axis.
19. **[Custom Interval for Both Axis]** – leave to default Auto. Interval controls the Axis value displayed on both Axis. 7 Interval on X-Axis will have 4 data points for a month and 12 for a year.
20. **[Log Scale]** – Log scales are automatically defined based on the Metrics value and will change both Left Y-Axis and Line position
21. **[Grid Configuration]** – leave this to default. This will automatically adapt the configurations based on your chart size and color. Consists of Axis Color, Grid Color, Font Family, Font Size, Label Font Size, Chart Backboard, and Border color:
22. **[Background and Border]** – customizable; Please refer to page 8 for a detailed explanation.
23. **[Legend]** – the default position is top. Other options are left, bottom, top, and none. Legend alignment (left, centre, right), Legend color, Font Family, Font Size, and Max Lines are also customizable. Please refer to page 13 for a detailed explanation.
24. **[Chart Header]** – chart headers allow viewers to perform several actions on charts, such as data export, drilling up or down, and view charts in explorer tools. Please refer to page 12 for a detailed explanation.

Recommended: Yes, See The Chart Version That Suits Your Need

- **Line Chart – Single Axis:** to trend over time.
- **Line Chart – Double-Axis:** to trend over time but if one of the data set compared is significantly smaller than the rest. Best practice to put those metrics on the second's Axis. Else line may a straight line on the X-Axis.
- **Sparkline:** by default, everything is unselected except the line representing the data. Most cases used just below a Scorecard later shown

III. Sparkline Chart:

Same as line chart and by default, everything is unselected except the line representing the data in Sparkline Chart. Most cases used just below a Scorecard shown below

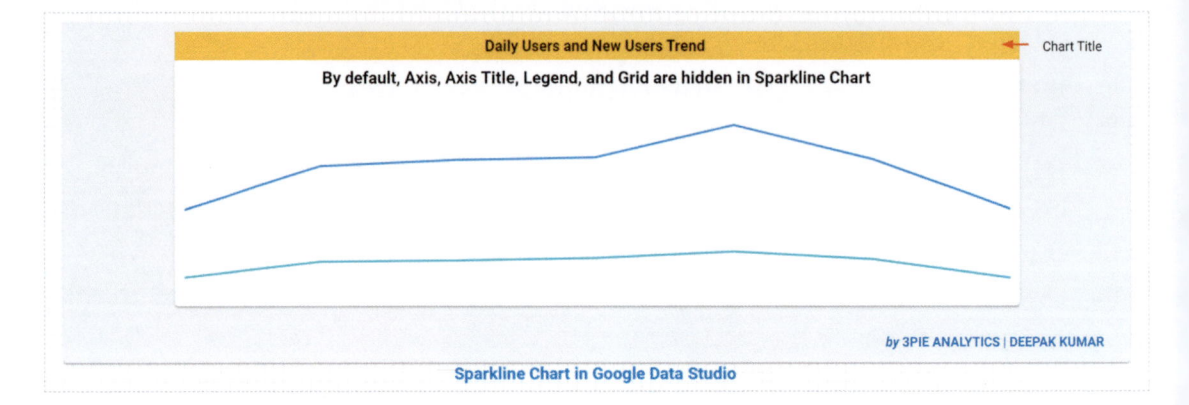

- In this chart, we display the Daily Users and New Users Trend

IV. How are Sparkline Charts Often used?

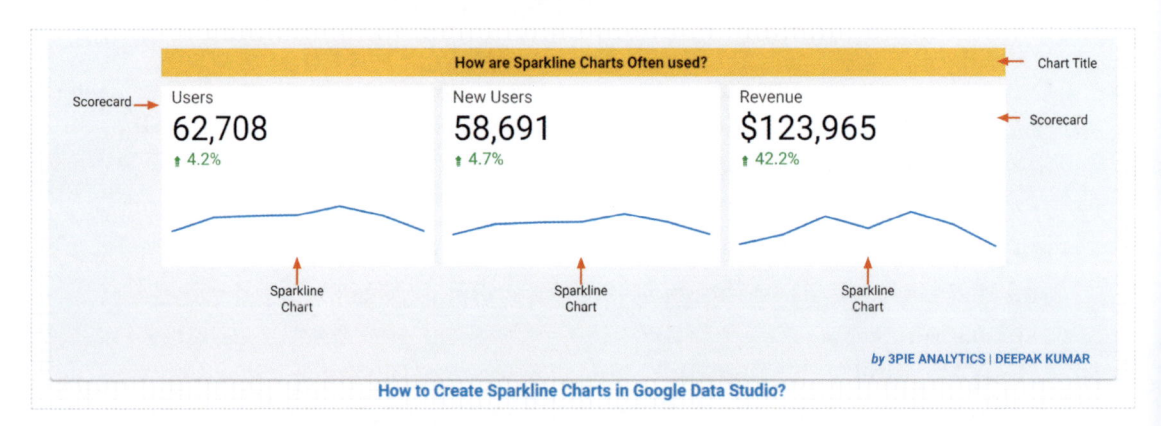

Configurations Available Within Sparkline Charts: Same As Line Chart

Page 58

V. Smoothed Time Series Chart:

Exactly the same as Line Chart, except Smooth is selected. Also Show Point is selected in this example and best to use this option if your time series is relatively small.

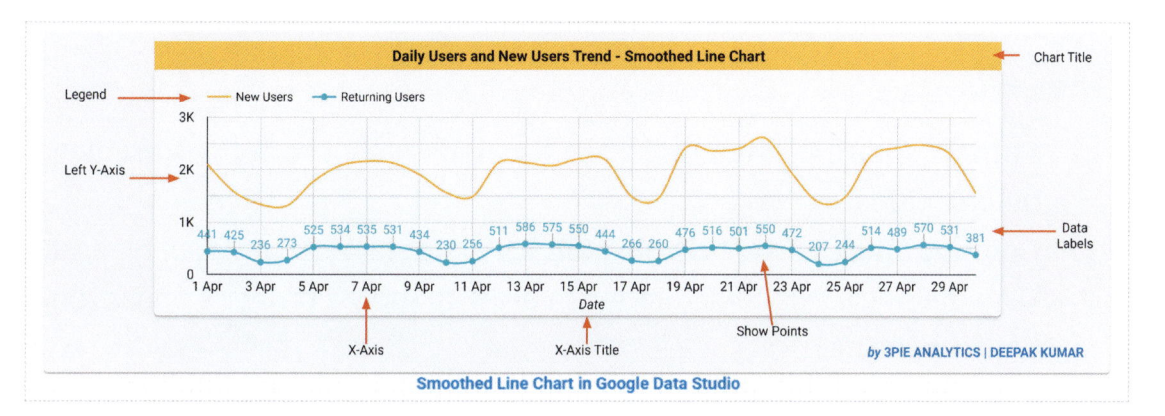

- In this chart, we display the Daily Users and New Users Trend

Configurations Available Within Smoothed Charts: Same As Line Chart

Chapter 7: Column Charts

A Column chart shows comparisons among discrete categories. One axis of the chart shows the specific categories being compared, and the other axis represents a measured value. The bars can be plotted vertically or horizontally.

Use case:

1. **Column Chart – Single Axis:** any data type to show comparison among different KPIs.
2. **Column Chart with Multiple Metrics – Single Axis:** any data type and keep the single axis configuration in order to show a proper comparison between the metrics
3. **Column Chart – Dual Axis:** suitable if both Axis data don't have significant differences or for displaying the "% of the total"

Recommended:

Yes, it is one of the most widely used charts across the industry.

Gauge Chart in Google Data Studio		
Chart Type	Axis	Recommended
Column Chart: Single Axis	Always	Yes
Multiple Metrics: Single Axis	Always	Yes
Column Chart: Dual Axis	Always	No
Stacked Column: Single Axis	Always	Yes
Stacked Column: Single Axis	Always	Yes
Stacked Column: Dual Axis	Always	No
100% Stacked Column	Always	Yes

Recommended Configurations For Column Charts:

1. **[Chart Title]** – the title is not absolutely necessary. Still, personally, I always prefer to have a title for each chart.
2. **[Number of Pubs/Bars]** – max 1000, and the number of pubs/bars should not be too large (the X-Axis label may appear incomplete).
3. **[Data Label]** – test the data label to see if it fits nicely for your column chart; if yes, display the data label as well.

4. **[Color by/Bar Color]** – individually customizable
5. **[Reference Line]** – add average reference lines to quickly identify the above average value
6. **[Reference Line Label]** – auto and individually customizable
7. **[X and Y-Axis]** – always show axis so users can correlate the bar data with both Axis
8. **[Axis Min and Max Value]** – leave this to default auto and will adjust the bar height automatically based on the metric value.
9. **[Legend]** – for a single axis column, chart legend is not necessary, but if your chart has more than one metric, always display Legend.

Others Configurations Available Within Column Charts:

10. **[Breakdown Dimension]** – in the DATA tab is only available if you have a single Metric configuration.
11. **[Column Chart Type]** – by default it's vertical but you can switch to horizontal bar charts
12. **[Metrics Compact Number and Decimal Precision]** – default displayed as a Raw number with auto decimal precision
13. **[Reference Line]** – please refer to page 14 for a detailed explanation.
14. **[X and Y-Axis Title]** – this is not necessary for a single Axis column chart or if you have legends, and will save some space for both Axis, especially if your chart is small.
15. **[Reverse X and Y-Axis]** – individually or both Axis can be reversed.
16. **[Log Scale]** – log scales are automatically defined based on the Metrics value and will affect both Left Y-Axis and Pub/bar size.
17. **[Grid Configuration]** – consists of Axis Color, Grid Color, Font Family, Font Size, Label Font Size, and Inner Chart Backboard & Border color.
18. **[Axis Font Color, Size and Family]** – leave to the default black. This works across the color palette.
19. **[Background and Border]** – customizable; please refer to page 8 for a detailed explanation.
20. **[Legend Position]** – default is top. Other options are none, right, and bottom.
21. **[Legend Alignment]** – default is left. Other options are center and right.
22. **[Chart Header and Font Color]** – chart headers allow viewers to perform several actions on charts, such as data export, drilling up or down, and view charts in explorer tools. Please refer to page 12 for a detailed explanation.

I. Column Chart: Single Axis

A Column/Bar chart shows comparisons among discrete categories. One axis of the chart shows the specific categories being compared, and the other axis represents a measured value. The bars can be plotted vertically or horizontally.

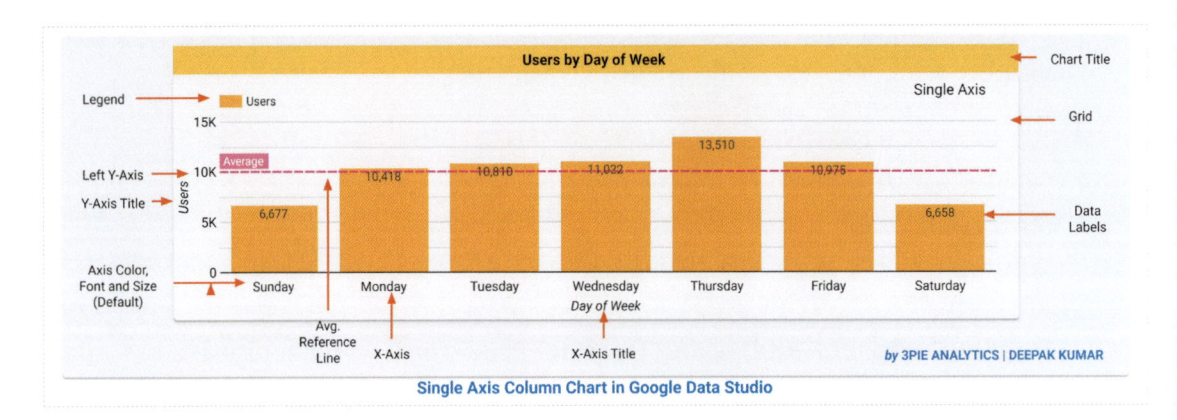

Single Axis Column Chart in Google Data Studio

- In this chart, we display users by weekday, with data aggregated by weekday for the selected time period.
- Adding an average reference will provide additional information about what to look for analysis. For example, in the above chart, we can analyze "Why are Thursday's average users 35% higher than the rest of the weekday?"

Chart Configurations:

1. **[Metric]** – Users
2. **[Chart Title]** – added in this example
3. **[Data Label]** – selected in this example and default is unselected
4. **[Color by/Bar Color]** – changed from default blue to Chrome Yellow
5. **[Reference Line]** – changed to Average from default Constant in this example
6. **[Reference Line Calculation]** – average
7. **[Reference Line Label]** – left to default auto "Average" in the above chart, but is customizable
8. **[Reference Line Color]** – changed to deep-pink from default black
9. **[X and Y-Axis Title]** – selected in this example and default is unselected
10. **[Background]** – this is gray in the above Scorecard, but the default will depend on how you have set up your theme.
11. **[Border Radius]** – 4 in this example
12. **[Border Color]** – this is transparent in this Scorecard, but the default will depend on how you have set up your theme.

13. **[Border Shadow]** – applied in the above charts. The default is not selected
14. **[Legend]** – for a single axis column, Legend is not necessary, but if your chart has more than one metric, always display Legend.

Other Configurations: Left To Default

15. **[Breakdown Dimension]** – in the DATA tab is only available if you have a single Metric configuration.
16. **[Number of Pubs/Bars]** – left to default 10
17. **[Metrics Compact Number and Decimal Precision]** – default unselected with auto decimal precision
18. **[Reference Line wight and Type]** – left to default 2px Dashed line
19. **[Axis]** – default, selected
20. **[Reverse X and Y-Axis]** – default, unselected
21. **[Log Scale]** – default, unselected
22. **[Grid Configuration]** – left to default
23. **[Axis, Font Color, Size and Family]** – theme default
24. **[Background Opacity]** – default is 100%
25. **[Border Weight and Style]** – default, none. Please refer to page 8 for a detailed explanation.
26. **[Chart Header and Font Color]** – chart headers allow viewers to perform several actions on charts, such as data export, drilling up or down, and view charts in explorer tools. Please refer to page 12 for a detailed explanation.

Recommended: Yes

– Yes, it is one of the most widely used charts across the industry.

II. Column Chart with Multiple Metrics: Single Axis

A Column chart shows comparisons among discrete categories. One axis of the chart shows the specific categories being compared, and the other axis represents a measured value. The bars can be plotted vertically or horizontally.

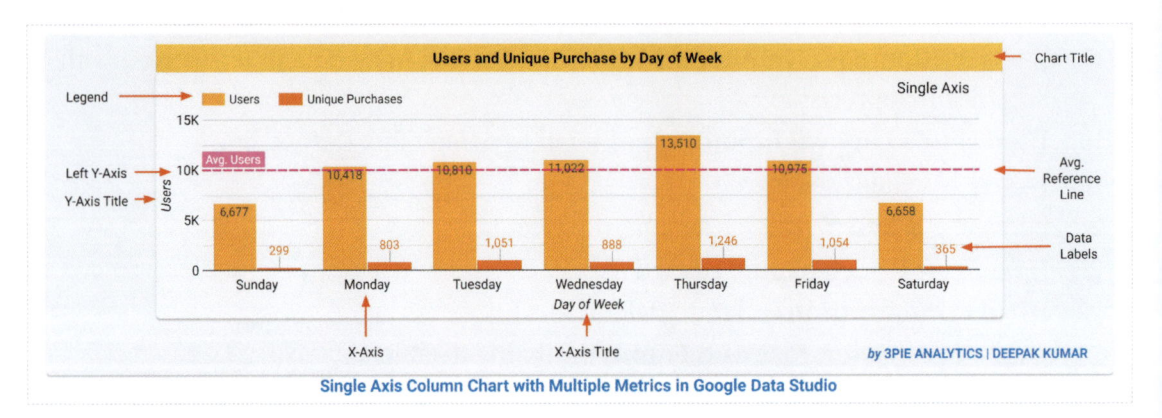

Single Axis Column Chart with Multiple Metrics in Google Data Studio

- In this chart, we display Users and Unique Purchases by weekday, with data aggregated by weekday for the selected time period.
- Adding an average reference will provide additional information about what to look for analysis. For example, in the above chart, we can analyze "Why are Thursday's average Users 35% higher than the rest of the weekday?"

Chart Configurations:
1. **[Metric]** – Users and Unique Purchases
2. **[Chart Title]** – added in this example
3. **[Data Label]** – selected in this example and default is unselected
4. **[Color by/Bar Color]** – changed from default blue to Chrome Yellow
5. **[Reference Line]** – changed to Average from default Constant in this example
6. **[Reference Line Calculation]** – average
7. **[Reference Line Label]** – changed to "Avg. Users". It's best practice to display the Reference label if you have more than one Metric, so your users can identify the corresponding Metric easily.
8. **[Reference Line Color]** – changed to deep-pink from default black
9. **[X and Y-Axis Title]** – selected in this example and default is unselected
10. **[Background]** – this is gray in the above Scorecard, but the default will depend on how you have set up your theme.
11. **[Border Radius]** – 4 in this example
12. **[Border Color]** – this is transparent in this Scorecard, but the default will depend on how you have set up your theme.

13. **[Border Shadow]** – applied in the above charts. The default is not selected
14. **[Legend]** – for a single axis column, chart legend is not necessary as well, but if your chart has more than one metric, always display Legend (see next example).

Other Configurations: Left To Default

15. **[Breakdown Dimension]** – not available if you have more than one Metric.
16. **[Number of Pubs/Bars]** – left to default 10
17. **[Metrics Compact Number and Decimal Precision]** – default unselected with auto decimal precision
18. **[Reference Line wight and Type]** – left to default 2px Dashed line
19. **[Axis]** – default, selected
20. **[Reverse X and Y-Axis]** – default, unselected
21. **[Log Scale]** – default, unselected
22. **[Grid Configuration]** – left to default
23. **[Axis, Font Color, Size and Family]** – theme default
24. **[Background Opacity]** – default is 100%
25. **[Border Weight and Style]** – default, none. Please refer to page 8 for a detailed explanation.
26. **[Chart Header and Font Color]** – chart headers allow viewers to perform several actions on charts, such as data export, drilling up or down, and view charts in explorer tools. Please refer to page 12 for a detailed explanation.

Recommended: Yes

- Yes, it is one of the most widely used charts across the industry.
- Keep the single axis configuration in order to show a proper comparison between the data set.

III. Column Chart: Dual Axis (1/2)

Suitable if both Axis data don't have significant differences or for displaying the "% of the total" for dual Axis column charts.

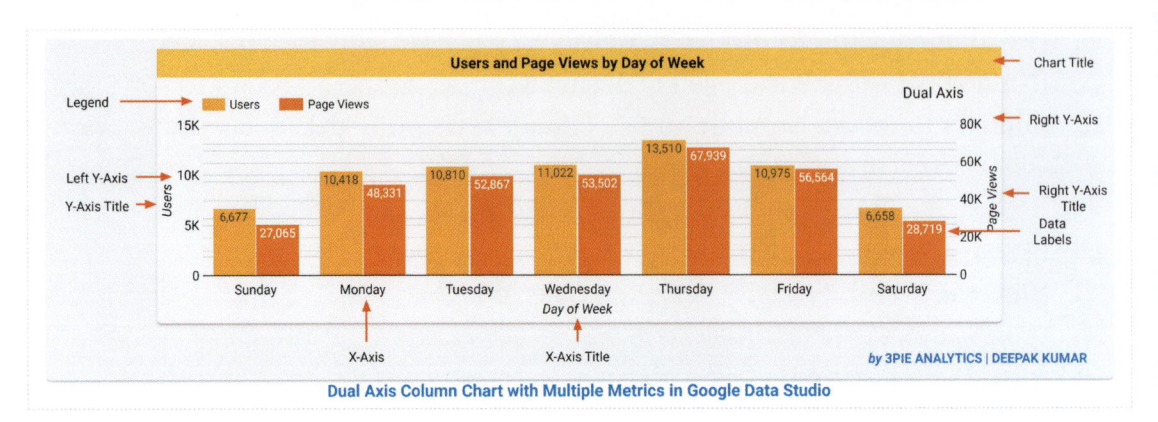

Dual Axis Column Chart with Multiple Metrics in Google Data Studio

- In this chart we display Users and Page Views by weekday. Data is aggregated by weekday for the selected time period.
- In this example, even where data has 3x-5x differences, they appear to have a difference of 10-15%. In the next example, we will change the "Absolute Value" to "% of Total."

Chart Configurations:

1. **[Metric]** – Users and Page Views
2. **[Chart Title]** – added in this example
3. **[Data Label]** – selected in this example and default is unselected
4. **[Color by/Bar Color]** – changed from default blue to Chrome Yellow
5. **[X and Y-Axis Title]** – selected in this example and default is unselected
6. **[Background]** – this is gray in the above Scorecard, but the default will depend on how you have set up your theme.
7. **[Border Radius]** – 4 in this example
8. **[Border Color]** – this is transparent in this Scorecard, but the default will depend on how you have set up your theme.
9. **[Border Shadow]** – applied in the above charts. The default is not selected
10. **[Legend]** – for multiple metrics column charts, always display Legends.

Other Configurations: Left To Default

11. **[Breakdown Dimension]** – not available if you have more than one Metric.
12. **[Number of Pubs/Bars]** – left to default 10
13. **[Metrics Compact Number and Decimal Precision]** – default unselected with auto decimal precision
14. **[Reference Line]** – none, please refer to page 14 for a detailed explanation.

15. **[Axis]** – default, selected
16. **[Reverse X and Y-Axis]** – default, unselected
17. **[Log Scale]** – default, unselected
18. **[Grid Configuration]** – left to default
19. **[Axis, Font Color, Size and Family]** – theme default
20. **[Background Opacity]** – default is 100%
21. **[Border Weight and Style]** – default, none. Please refer to page 8 for a detailed explanation.
22. **[Chart Header and Font Color]** – chart headers allow viewers to perform several actions on charts, such as data export, drilling up or down, and view charts in explorer tools. Please refer to page 12 for a detailed explanation.

Recommended: No

- For most audiences, it's hard to make intuitively correct statements about two data series which have a significant difference.
- In this example, even where data has 3x-5x differences, they appear to have a difference of 10-15%. In the following example, we will change the "Absolute Value" to "% of Total."

IV. Column Chart: Dual Axis (2/2)

Suitable if both Axis data don't have significant differences or for displaying the "% of the total" for dual Axis column charts.

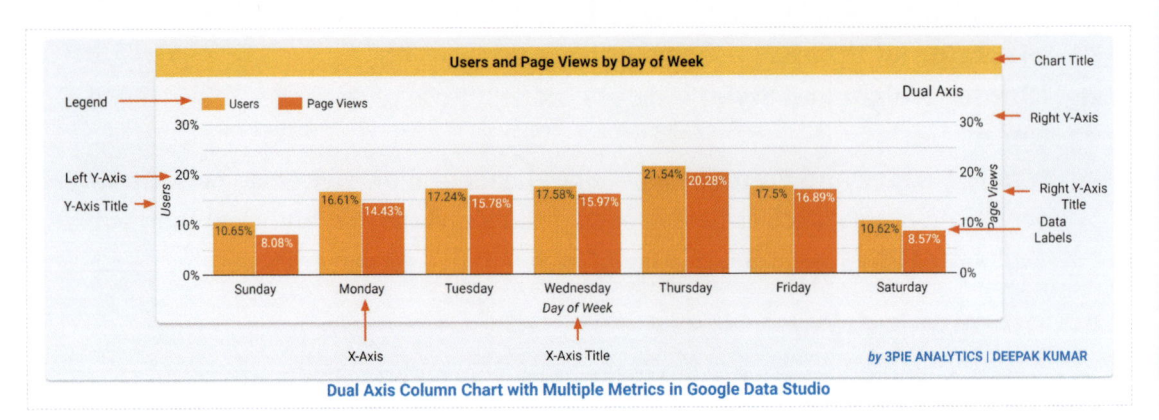

Dual Axis Column Chart with Multiple Metrics in Google Data Studio

- In this chart we display Users and Page Views by weekday. Data is aggregated by weekday for the selected time period.
- In this example, we have changed "Absolute Value" to "% of Total." Thus, both Users and Page Views become visually comparable.

Chart Configurations:

1. **[Metric]** – Users and Page Views
2. **[Chart Title]** – added in this example
3. **[Data Label]** – selected in this example and default is unselected
4. **[Color by/Bar Color]** – changed from default blue to Chrome Yellow
5. **[X and Y-Axis Title]** – selected in this example and default is unselected
6. **[Background]** – this is gray in the above Scorecard, but the default will depend on how you have set up your theme.
7. **[Border Radius]** – 4 in this example
8. **[Border Color]** – this is transparent in this Scorecard, but the default will depend on how you have set up your theme.
9. **[Border Shadow]** – applied in the above charts. The default is not selected
10. **[Legend]** – for multiple metrics column charts, always display Legends.

Other Configurations: Left To Default

11. **[Breakdown Dimension]** – not available if you have more than one Metric.
12. **[Number of Pubs/Bars]** – left to default 10
13. **[Metrics Compact Number and Decimal Precision]** – default unselected with auto decimal precision
14. **[Reference Line]** – none, please refer to page 14 for a detailed explanation.
15. **[Axis]** – default, selected

16. **[Reverse X and Y Axis]** – default, unselected
17. **[Log Scale]** – default, unselected
18. **[Grid Configuration]** – left to default
19. **[Axis, Font Color, Size and Family]** – theme default
20. **[Background Opacity]** – default is 100%
21. **[Border Weight and Style]** – default, none. Please refer to page 8 for a detailed explanation.
22. **[Chart Header and Font Color]** – chart headers allow viewers to perform several actions on charts, such as data export, drilling up or down, and view charts in explorer tools. Please refer to page 12 for a detailed explanation.

Recommended: Yes

- Suitable if both Axis data set don't have a significant difference or display the "% of the total" in a dual Axis column chart.

V. Stacked Column: Single Axis

Stacked Columns represent multiple types of data within a single bar stacked vertically, one on top of another. The value determines the length of each series in each data point.

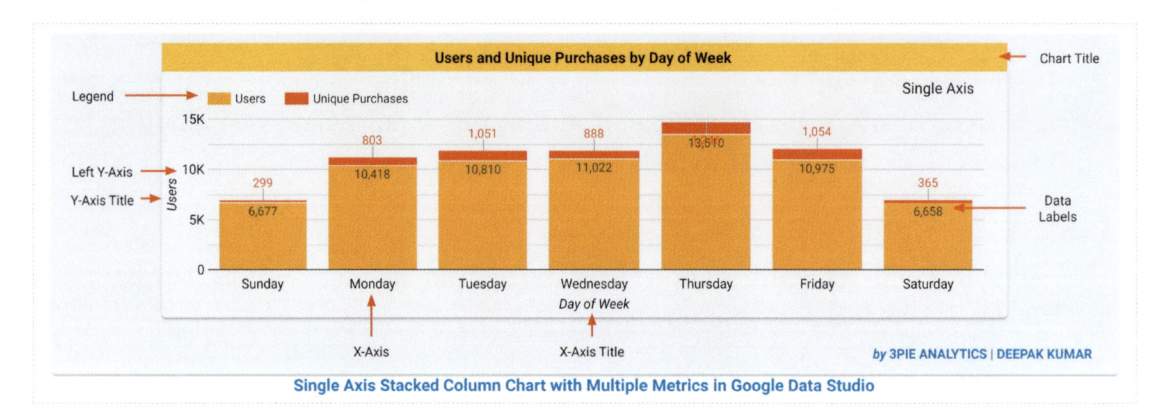

Single Axis Stacked Column Chart with Multiple Metrics in Google Data Studio

- In this chart we display Users and Unique Purchases by weekday. Data is aggregated by weekday for the selected time period. For example, in this chart, "What are the weekday Unique Purchases against Total Users?"

Chart Configurations:

1. **[Metrics]** – it's best practice to use only two or three metrics as too many will make it very hard to see patterns in the data. **A Double Axis configuration is only available for up to two metrics inside the Stacked Column chart.**
2. **[Chart Title]** – added in this example
3. **[Data Label]** – selected in this example and default is unselected
4. **[Color by/Bar Color]** – changed from default blue to Chrome Yellow
5. **[X and Y-Axis Title]** – selected in this example and default is unselected
6. **[Background]** – this is gray in the above Scorecard, but the default will depend on how you have set up your theme.
7. **[Border Radius]** – 4 in this example
8. **[Border Color]** – this is transparent in this Scorecard, but the default will depend on how you have set up your theme.
9. **[Border Shadow]** – applied in the above charts. The default is not selected
10. **[Legend]** – for multiple metrics column charts, always display Legends.

Other Configurations: Left To Default

11. **[Breakdown Dimension]** – not available if you have more than one Metric.
12. **[Number of Pubs/Bars]** – left to default 10
13. **[Metrics Compact Number and Decimal Precision]** – default unselected with auto decimal precision

14. **[Reference Line]** – none, please refer to page 14 for a detailed explanation.
15. **[Reference Line Type]** – only Constant and Parameter is available within the Stacked Column Chart.
16. **[Axis]** – default, selected
17. **[Reverse X and Y-Axis]** – default, unselected
18. **[Log Scale]** – default, unselected
19. **[Grid Configuration]** – left to default
20. **[Axis, Font Color, Size and Family]** – theme default
21. **[Background Opacity]** – default is 100%
22. **[Border Weight and Style]** – default, none. Please refer to page 8 for a detailed explanation.
23. **[Chart Header and Font Color]** – chart headers allow viewers to perform several actions on charts, such as data export, drilling up or down, and view charts in explorer tools. Please refer to page 12 for a detailed explanation.

Recommended: Yes

- Stacked Column Charts are a great choice if you need to observe how each of the individual variables and their sums change.
- Double axis configurations are not recommended for Stacked Column Charts, as visual comparison between the data sets will be tough to comprehend for most users. In the following chart, we will display the same chart with a Double Axis configuration.

VI. Stacked Column: Dual Axis

Stacked Columns represent multiple types of data within a single bar stacked vertically, one on top of another. The value determines the length of each series in each data point.

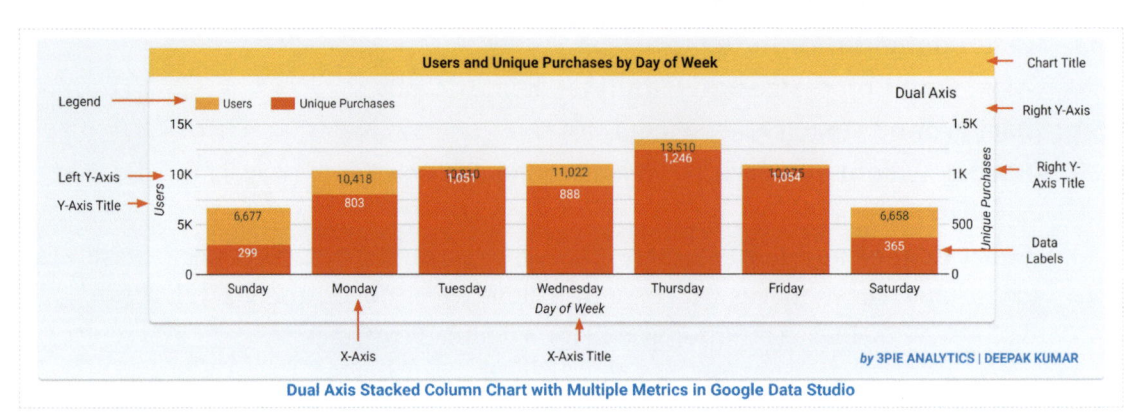

Dual Axis Stacked Column Chart with Multiple Metrics in Google Data Studio

- In this chart, we display Users and Unique Purchases by weekday, and data is aggregated by weekday for the selected time period.
- When we changed to Double Axis configuration, the Stacked bar distribution doesn't make sense. It's best to avoid double axis for a Stacked Column Chart.

Chart Configurations:

1. **[Metrics]** – it is best practice to use only two or three metrics as too many will make it very hard to see patterns in the data. **A Double Axis configuration is only available for up to two metrics inside the Stacked Column chart.**
2. **[Chart Title]** –added in this example
3. **[Data Label]** – selected in this example and default is unselected
4. **[Color by/Bar Color]** – changed from default blue to Chrome Yellow
5. **[X and Y-Axis Title]** – selected in this example and default is unselected
6. **[Background]** – this is gray in the above Scorecard, but the default will depend on how you have set up your theme.
7. **[Border Radius]** – 4 in this example
8. **[Border Color]** – this is transparent in this Scorecard, but the default will depend on how you have set up your theme.
9. **[Border Shadow]** – applied in the above charts. The default is not selected
10. **[Legend]** – for multiple metrics column charts, always display Legends.

Other Configurations: Left To Default

11. **[Breakdown Dimension]** – not available if you have more than one Metric.
12. **[Number of Pubs/Bars]** – left to default 10

13. **[Metrics Compact Number and Decimal Precision]** – default unselected with auto decimal precision
14. **[Reference Line]** – none
15. **[Reference Line Type]** – only Constant and Parameter is available within the Stacked Column Chart.
16. **[Axis]** – default, selected
17. **[Reverse X and Y-Axis]** – default, unselected
18. **[Log Scale]** – default, unselected
19. **[Grid Configuration]** – left to default
20. **[Axis, Font Color, Size and Family]** – theme default
21. **[Background Opacity]** – default is 100%
22. **[Border Weight and Style]** – default, none. Please refer to page 8 for a detailed explanation.
23. **[Chart Header and Font Color]** – chart headers allow viewers to perform several actions on charts, such as data export, drilling up or down, and view charts in explorer tools. Please refer to page 12 for a detailed explanation.

Recommended: No

- Double axis configurations are not recommended for Stacked Column Charts, as visual comparison between the data sets will be tough to comprehend for most users.

VII. 100% Stacked Column (1/2)

100% Stacked Column Charts are a great choice if you need to observe how each of the individual shares changes over time.

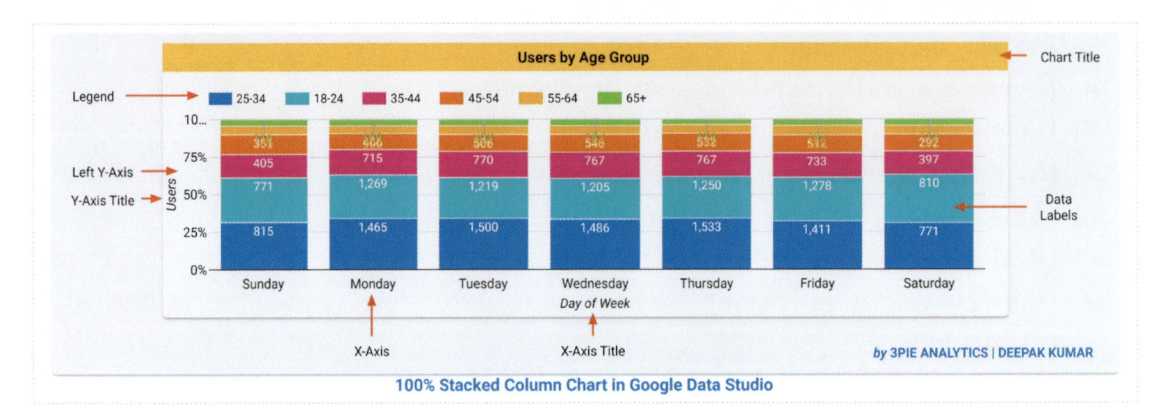

- In this chart we display Users by Age Group, and data is aggregated by weekday for the selected time period.
- Even though 100% stacked columns always equal 100%, it's best to have % data within the chart, so your audience can see the actual % by showing the data label. Otherwise, it can be difficult to compare the relative size of each component visually. In the following chart, we will display the same data as "% of Total."

Chart Configurations:
1. **[Breakdown Dimension]** – selected in the DATA tab. 100% Stacked column chart should a show Breakdown Dimension, otherwise it would be a standard Column Chart.
2. **[Metrics]** – in a 100% Stacked column chart, only one Metric is allowed.
3. **[Data Label]** – selected in this example and default is unselected
4. **[Color by/Bar Color]** – changed from default blue to Chrome Yellow
5. **[X and Y-Axis Title]** – selected in this example and default is unselected
6. **[Background]** – this is gray in the above Scorecard, but the default will depend on how you have set up your theme.
7. **[Border Radius]** – 4 in this example
8. **[Border Color]** – this is transparent in this Scorecard, but the default will depend on how you have set up your theme.
9. **[Border Shadow]** – applied in the above charts. The default is not selected
10. **[Legend]** – always display Legends in 100% stacked column charts.

Other Configurations: Left To Default
11. **[Number of Pubs/Bars]** – left to default 10

Page 74

12. **[Metrics Compact Number and Decimal Precision]** – default unselected with auto decimal precision
13. **[Reference Line]** – not available for 100% Stacked Column Chart.
14. **[Axis]** – default, selected
15. **[Reverse X and Y-Axis]** – default, unselected
16. **[Log Scale]** – default, unselected
17. **[Grid Configuration]** – left to default
18. **[Axis, Font Color, Size and Family]** – theme default
19. **[Background Opacity]** – default is 100%
20. **[Border Weight and Style]** – default, none. Please refer to page 8 for a detailed explanation.
21. **[Chart Header and Font Color]** – chart headers allow viewers to perform several actions on charts, such as data export, drilling up or down, and view charts in explorer tools. Please refer to page 12 for a detailed explanation.

Recommended: Yes

- 100% Stacked Column Charts are a great choice if you need to observe how each of the individual shares changes over time.

VIII. 100% Stacked Column (2/2)

100% Stacked Column Charts are a great choice if you need to observe how each of the individual shares changes over time.

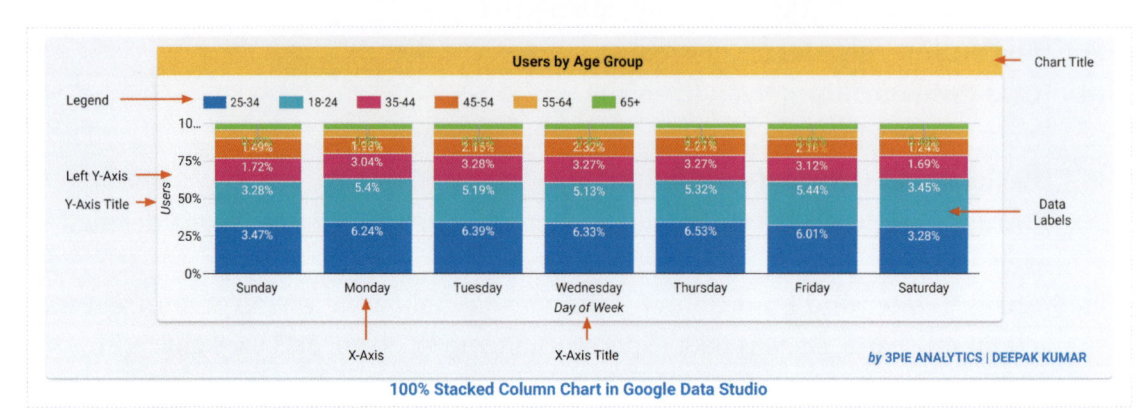

100% Stacked Column Chart in Google Data Studio

- In this chart, we display Users by Age Group, and data is aggregated by weekday for the selected time period.
- In this chart, we are displaying the previous chart data as "% of Total."

Chart Configurations:

1. **[Breakdown Dimension]** – selected in the DATA tab. 100% Stacked column chart should a show Breakdown Dimension, otherwise it would be a standard Column Chart.
2. **[Metrics]** – in a 100% Stacked column chart, only one Metric is allowed.
3. **[Metrics - calculation]** – Comparison calculation changed from None to "Percent of total => Relative to corresponding data."
4. **[Data Label]** – selected in this example and default is unselected
5. **[Color by/Bar Color]** – changed from default blue to Chrome Yellow
6. **[X and Y-Axis Title]** – selected in this example and default is unselected
7. **[Background]** – this is gray in the above Scorecard, but the default will depend on how you have set up your theme.
8. **[Border Radius]** – 4 in this example
9. **[Border Color]** – this is transparent in this Scorecard, but the default will depend on how you have set up your theme.
10. **[Border Shadow]** – applied in the above charts. The default is not selected
11. **[Legend]** – always display Legends in 100% stacked column charts.

Other Configurations: Left To Default

12. **[Number of Pubs/Bars]** – left to default 10
13. **[Metrics Compact Number and Decimal Precision]** – default unselected with auto decimal precision

14. **[Reference Line]** – not available for 100% Stacked Column Chart.
15. **[Axis]** – default, selected
16. **[Reverse X and Y-Axis]** – default, unselected
17. **[Log Scale]** – default, unselected
18. **[Grid Configuration]** – left to default
19. **[Axis, Font Color, Size and Family]** – theme default
20. **[Background Opacity]** – default is 100%
21. **[Border Weight and Style]** – default, none. Please refer to page 8 for a detailed explanation.
22. **[Chart Header and Font Color]** – chart headers allow viewers to perform several actions on charts, such as data export, drilling up or down, and view charts in explorer tools. Please refer to page 12 for a detailed explanation.

Recommended: Yes

- 100% Stacked Column Charts are a great choice if you need to observe how each of the individual shares changes over time.

Chapter 8: Combo Charts

Combo charts use both axes to show a comparison between different KPIs. They work in a similar way to Column charts except with the option to configure how to display individual metrics (Line and Pub/Bar). The right axis is often used, If a data set is significantly smaller than the rest of the KPIs.

Use case:

1. **Combo Chart: Single Axis** – Single Axis configuration works well if the metrics you are comparing have at least a 3-5% difference.
2. **Combo Chart: Dual Axis** – Always use double Axis configuration, If one of your data sets is significantly smaller than the rest of the KPIs.

Recommended: Yes

Unless X-Axis is a date, keep the number of pubs/bars to a max of 15.

Combo Chart in Google Data Studio			
Chart Type	X and Y-Axis	X and Y-Axis Title	Recommended
Combo Chart: Single Axis	Always	Always	Yes
Combo Chart: Dual Axis	Always	Always	Yes (Personal fav)
Stacked Combo Chart: Single Axis	Always	Always	Yes
Stacked Combo Chart: Dual Axis	Always	Always	Yes

Recommended Configurations For Combo Charts:

1. **[Metrics]** – it's best practice to use only two or three metrics as too many will make it very hard to see patterns in the data. Maximum 20 metrics and one dimension allowed in a Combo Chart
2. **[Chart Title]** – title is not necessary, but personally, I always prefer to have a title for each chart.
3. **[Dual Axis configuration]** – if one of the metrics values is significantly smaller than other metrics.
4. **[Small value KPI on the right Y-Axis]** – personal preference

5. **[Data Label]** – test the data label to see if it fits nicely for your chart; if yes, display the data label as well.
6. **[Number of Points]** – 500 Default, the number of pubs/bars should not be too large (the X-Axis label may appear incomplete).
7. **[Axes]** – always display both Axis for all combo charts
8. **[X and Y-Axis Title]** – display at least Y-Axis title for dual Axis configuration so the audience can quickly identify metrics displayed on both sides.
9. **[Axis Min & Max Value and Custom Interval]** – leave this to default auto and will adjust the bar height automatically based on the metric value.
10. **[Legend]** – a Combo chart should have more than one metric, or it would be a usual Column Chart, and best practice to display the legends.

Others Configurations Available Within Combo Charts:

11. **[Series Color]** – individually customizable
12. **[Series Axis]** – individually selected to display either on the left or right axis
13. **[Series Number]** – this can be configured individually for either Line or Bar charts and should be displayed on either the left or right Axis.
14. **[Line Smooth]** – default unselected
15. **[Number of Points]** – 500 Default and max 1000, the number of data points
16. **[Series Number Format]** – Individual series (selected metrics of your chart) can be displayed as Cumulative or Compact Numbers with a decimal precision
17. **[Reference Line]** – reference lines will be automatically created based on the Metrics value, and a max of ten reference lines are allowed. Please refer to page 14 for a detailed explanation.
18. **[Reverse X and Y-Axis]** – individually or both Axis can be reversed.
19. **[Log Scale]** – Log scales are automatically defined based on the Metrics value and will change both Left Y-Axis and Pub/bar size
20. **[Grid Configuration]** – consists of Axis Color, Grid Color, Font Family, Font Size, Label Font Size, and Inner Chart Backboard & Border color.
21. **[Axis Font Color, Size and Family]** – leave to the default black. This works across the color palette.
22. **[Background and Border]** – customizable; Please refer to page 8 for a detailed explanation.
23. **[Legend Position]** – default is top. Other options are none, right, and bottom.
24. **[Legend Alignment]** – default is left. Other options are center and right.
25. **[Chart Header and Font Color]** – chart headers allow viewers to perform several actions on charts, such as data export, drilling up or down, and view charts in explorer tools. Please refer to page 12 for a detailed explanation.

I. Combo Chart: Double Axis

Combo charts use both axes to show a comparison between different KPIs. They work in a similar way to Column charts except with the option to configure how to display individual metrics (Line and Pub/Bar). The right axis is often used if a data set is significantly smaller than the rest of the KPIs - for example, Revenue per User as shown in the chart below.

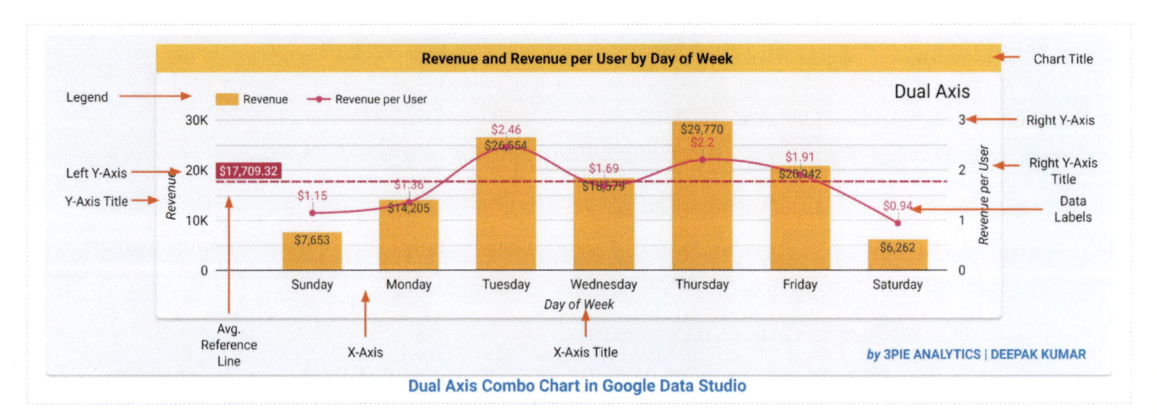

Dual Axis Combo Chart in Google Data Studio

- In this chart, we display Users and Revenue per User by weekday. Data is aggregated by weekday for the selected time period.
- Adding an average reference will provide additional information about what to look for during analysis. For example, in the above chart, we can analyze "Why is Thursday's average Revenue 71% higher than the rest of the week?"

Chart Configurations:

1. **[Metrics]** – it's best practice to use only two or three metrics as too many will make it very hard to see patterns in the data. Maximum 20 metrics and one dimension allowed in a Combo Chart
2. **[Chart Title]** – added in this example. Title is not necessary, but personally, I always prefer to have a title for each chart.
3. **[Series Color/Bar Color]** – changed from default blue to Chrome Yellow
4. **[Data Label]** – selected in this example for both series and default is unselected. Test for the data label if it fits nicely; if yes, display the data label as well
5. **[Series Axis]** – individually selected to display either on the left or right axis
6. **[Series Number]** – Revenue is "Series no. 1" in the above example. Configure individually for either Line or Bar chart and display it either on the left or right Axis.
7. **[Line Smooth]** – selected for this chart, personal preference

8. **[Number of Points]** – 500 Default, the number of pubs/bars should not be too large (the X-Axis label may appear incomplete). Unless X-Axis is a date, keep the number of points to a max of 15.
9. **[Reference Line]** – average revenue in this example, and metrics available as a dropdown list
10. **[Axes]** – always display both Axis for all combo charts
11. **[X and Y-Axis Title]** – display at least Y-Axis title for dual Axis configuration so the audience can quickly identify metrics displayed on both sides.
12. **[Background]** – this is gray in the above Scorecard, but the default will depend on how you have set up your theme.
13. **[Border Radius]** – 4 in this example
14. **[Border Color]** – this is transparent in this chart, but the default will depend on how you have set up your theme.
15. **[Border Shadow]** – applied in the above charts. The default is not selected
16. **[Legend]** – a Combo chart should have more than one metric, or it would be a usual Column Chart, and best practice to display the legends if your chart has more than one metric.

Other Configurations: Left To Default

17. **[Series Number Format]** – individual series (selected metrics of your chart) can be displayed as Cumulative or Compact Numbers with a decimal precision
18. **[Reference Line]** – max ten reference lines are allowed
19. **[Reverse X and Y-Axis]** – individually or both Axis can be reversed. If we reverse the X-Axis in this example, Saturday will show first instead of Sunday
20. **[Axis Min & Max Value and Custom Interval]** – leave this to default auto and will adjust the bar height automatically based on the metric value.
21. **[Log Scale]** – Log scales are automatically defined based on the Metrics value and will change both Left Y-Axis and Pub/bar size
22. **[Grid Configuration]** – consists of Axis Color, Grid Color, Font Family, Font Size, Label Font Size, Chart Backboard, and Border color.
23. **[Background and Border]** – customizable; please refer to page 8 for a detailed explanation.
24. **[Legend]** – the default position is top. Other options are left, bottom, top, and none. Please refer to page 13 for a detailed explanation.
25. **[Chart Header]** – please refer to page 12 for a detailed explanation.

Recommended: Yes

- Unless X-Axis is a date, keep the number of pubs/bars to a max of 15.
- Always use a double Axis configuration if one of your data sets is significantly smaller than the rest of the KPIs. Display smaller value metrics on the right Axis.

II. Combo Chart: Single Axis

A Single Axis configuration works well if the metrics you are comparing have at least a 3-5% difference. For example, if we compare Users and Revenue per User in the below chart, the Revenue per User data will be a straight line on the bottom of the X-Axis.

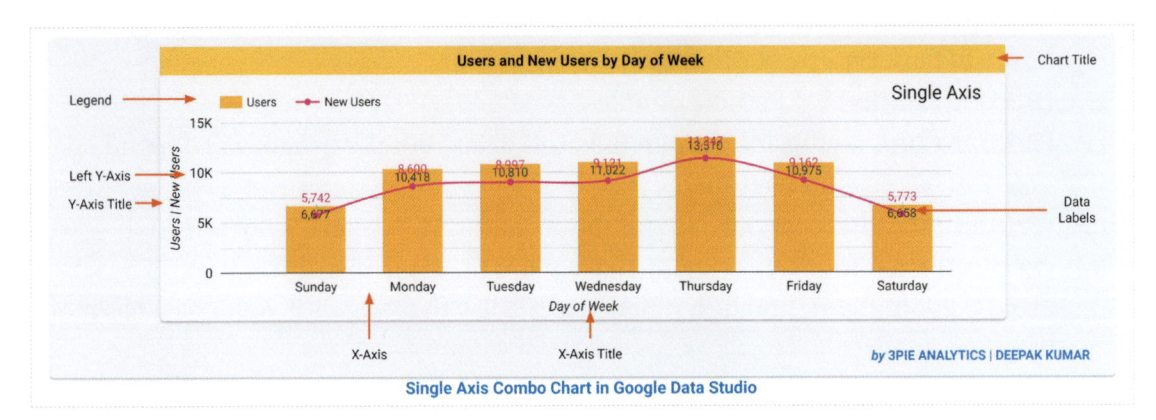

Single Axis Combo Chart in Google Data Studio

– In this chart we display Users and New Users by weekday, and data is aggregated by weekday for the selected period.

Chart Configurations:

1. **[Metrics]** – it's best practice to use only two or three metrics as too many will make it very hard to see patterns in the data. Maximum 20 metrics and one dimension allowed in a Combo Chart
2. **[Chart Title]** – added in this example. In a Combo chart, you have the option to display both Axis together with Legend, and the title is not necessary, but personally, I always prefer to have a title for each chart.
3. **[Series Color/Bar Color]** – changed from default blue to Chrome Yellow
4. **[Data Label]** – selected in this example for both series and default is unselected. Test for the data label if it fits nicely; if yes, display the data label as well
5. **[Series Axis]** – individually selected to display either on the left or right axis
6. **[Series Number]** – Users is "Series no. 1" in the above example. This can be configured individually for either Line or Bar charts and should be displayed on either the left or right axis.
7. **[Line Smooth]** – selected for this chart, personal preference
8. **[Number of Points]** – 500 Default, the number of pubs/bars should not be too large (the X-Axis label may appear incomplete). Unless X-Axis is a date, keep the number of points to a max of 15.
9. **[Axes]** – always display both Axis for all combo charts

10. **[X and Y-Axis Title]** – display at least Y-Axis title for dual Axis configuration so the audience can quickly identify metrics displayed on both sides.
11. **[Background]** – this is gray in the above Scorecard, but the default will depend on how you have set up your theme.
12. **[Border Radius]** – 4 in this example
13. **[Border Color]** – this is transparent in this chart, but the default will depend on how you have set up your theme.
14. **[Border Shadow]** – applied in the above charts. The default is not selected
15. **[Legend]** – a Combo chart should have more than one metric, or it would be a usual Column Chart, and best practice to display the legends if your chart has more than one metric.

Other Configurations: Left To Default

16. **[Series Number Format]** – individual series (selected metrics of your chart) can be displayed as Cumulative or Compact Numbers with a decimal precision
17. **[Reference Line]** – none, max ten reference lines are allowed.
18. **[Reverse X and Y-Axis]** – individually or both Axis can be reversed. If we reverse the X-Axis for the above chart, Saturday will show first instead of Sunday
19. **[Axis Min & Max Value and Custom Interval]** – leave this to default auto and will adjust the bar height automatically based on the metric value.
20. **[Log Scale]** – Log scales are automatically defined based on the Metrics value and will change both Left Y-Axis and Pub/bar size
21. **[Breakdown Dimension]** – not available for a Combo Chart
22. **[Grid Configuration]** – consists of Axis Color, Grid Color, Font Family, Font Size, Label Font Size, Chart Backboard, and Border color.
23. **[Background and Border]** – customizable; please refer to page 8 for a detailed explanation.
24. **[Legend]** – the default position is top. Other options are left, bottom, top, and none. Please refer to page 13 for a detailed explanation.
25. **[Chart Header]** – chart headers allow viewers to perform several actions on charts, such as data export, drilling up or down, and view charts in explorer tools. Please refer to page 12 for a detailed explanation.

Recommended: Yes

- Unless X-Axis is a date, it's recommend to keep the number of pubs/bars to a maximum of 15.
- A Single Axis configuration works well if the metrics you are comparing have at least a 3-5% difference. In the next example we will use a Single Axis configuration for the Stacked Combo chart to see how it compares

III. Stacked Combo Chart: Single Axis

Stacked Combo charts represent multiple data types within a single bar and are ideal for comparing the total value across each group/segmented bar. This value determines the length of each series in each data point.

These charts work in a similar way to Column chart except you can configure how you choose to display (Line and Pub/Bar) individual metrics. In the below example, the line representing the Revenue per User would not be possible to configure in a Column chart.

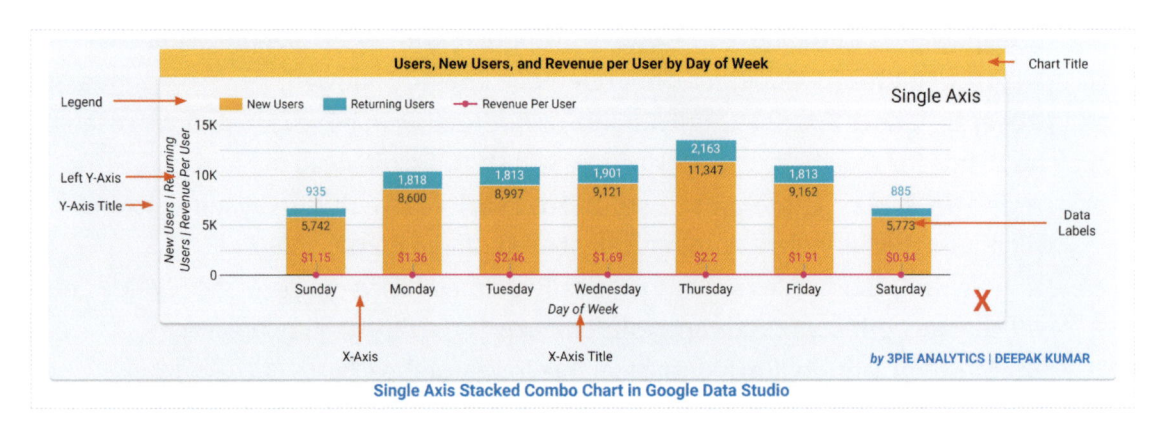

Single Axis Stacked Combo Chart in Google Data Studio

- In this chart we are comparing Users, Returning Users and Revenue per User against the total. The Revenue per User line is a straight line on the bottom of X-Axis. This is why you should always use a double Axis configuration when one of the metrics you are comparing is significantly smaller than the rest of the metrics.

Chart Configurations:

1. **[Metrics]** – it's best practice to use only two or three metrics as too many will make it very hard to see patterns in the data. Maximum 20 metrics and one dimension allowed in a Combo Chart
2. **[Chart Title]** – title is not necessary, but personally, I always prefer to have a title for each chart.
3. **[Series Color/Bar Color]** – changed from default blue to Chrome Yellow
4. **[Data Label]** – selected in this example for both series and default is unselected. Test for the data label if it fits nicely; if yes, display the data label as well
5. **[Series Axis]** – only for line chart configuration and displayed either on the left or right axis

6. **[Series Number]** – in a Stake Combo Chart, Bars are always displayed on the left. Line Chart (Revenue per User in the above example) can be displayed either left or right Axis.
7. **[Number of Points]** – 500 by default, and the number of pubs/bars should not be too large as the X-Axis label may appear incomplete. Unless X-Axis is a date, keep the number of points to a max of 15.
8. **[Axes]** – always display both Axis for all combo charts
9. **[X and Y-Axis Title]** – not necessary for a single Axis Combo chart, and will save some space for both Axis, especially your chart is small
10. **[Background]** – this is gray in the above Scorecard, but the default will depend on how you have set up your theme.
11. **[Border Radius]** – 4 in this example
12. **[Border Color]** – this is transparent in this chart
13. **[Border Shadow]** – applied in the above charts. The default is not selected
14. **[Legend]** – a Combo chart should have more than one metric, or it would be a usual Column Chart, and best practice to display the legends if your chart has more than one metric.

Other Configurations: Left To Default

15. **[Series Number Format]** – individual series (selected metrics of your chart) can be displayed as Cumulative or Compact Numbers with a decimal precision
16. **[Line Smooth]** – unselected
17. **[Reference Line]** – none, max ten reference lines are allowed. Please refer to page 13 for a detailed explanation.
18. **[Reverse X and Y-Axis]** – individually or both Axis can be reversed.
19. **[Axis Min & Max Value and Custom Interval]** – leave this to default auto and will adjust the bar height automatically based on the metric value.
20. **[Log Scale]** – Log scales are automatically defined based on the Metrics value and will change both Left Y-Axis and Pub/bar size
21. **[Grid Configuration]** – consists of Axis Color, Grid Color, Font Family, Font Size, Label Font Size, Chart Backboard, and Border color.
22. **[Background and Border]** – customizable; please refer to page 8 for a detailed explanation.
23. **[Legend]** – the default position is top. Other options are left, bottom, top, and none. Please refer to page 13 for a detailed explanation.
24. **[Chart Header]** – please refer to page 12 for a detailed explanation.

Recommended: No

- A Single Axis configuration works well if the metrics you are comparing have a difference of at least 3-5%.

IV. Stacked Combo Chart: Dual Axis

Stacked Combo charts represent multiple types of data within a single bar and are ideal for comparing the total value across each group/segmented bar. The value determines the length of each series in each data point.

Works similar way as Column chart except you can configure how you want to display (Line and Pub/Bar) individual metric.

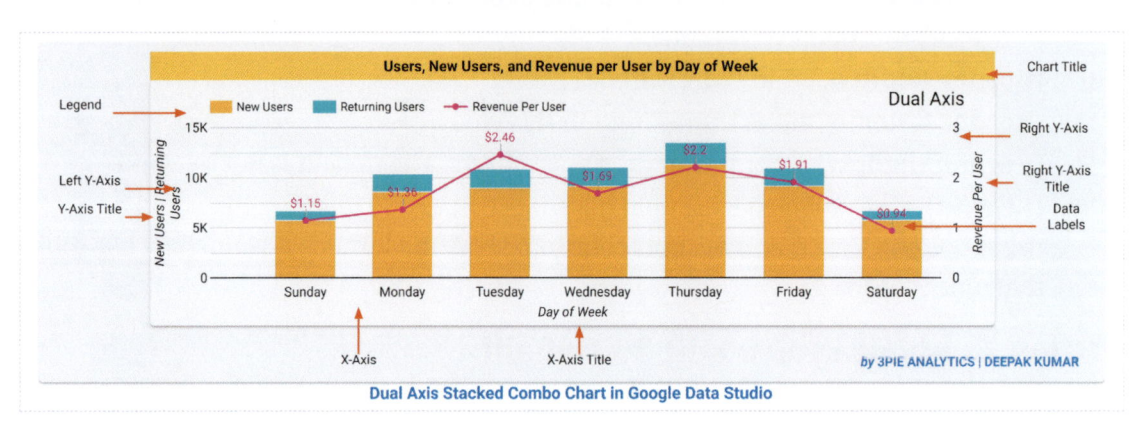

Dual Axis Stacked Combo Chart in Google Data Studio

– In this chart we are comparing Users and New Users Revenue per User against the total. In the double Axis configuration, we can also see the trend for the smaller data series. This is why you should always use a dual Axis configuration if one of the metrics you are comparing is significantly smaller than the rest of the set.

Chart Configurations:

1. **[Metrics]** – it's best practice to use only two or three metrics as too many will make it very hard to see patterns in the data. Maximum 20 metrics and one dimension allowed in a Combo Chart
2. **[Chart Title]** – title is not necessary, but personally, I always prefer to have a title for each chart.
3. **[Series Color/Bar Color]** – changed from default blue to Chrome Yellow
4. **[Data Label]** – selected in this example for both series and default is unselected. Test for the data label if it fits nicely; if yes, display the data label as well
5. **[Series Axis]** – only for line chart configuration and displayed either on the left or right axis
6. **[Series Number]** – in a Stake Combo Chart, Bars are always displayed on the left. Line Chart (Revenue per User in the above example) can be displayed either left or right Axis.

7. **[Number of Points]** – 500 Default, the number of pubs/bars should not be too large (the X-Axis label may appear incomplete). Unless X-Axis is a date, keep the number of points to a max of 15.
8. **[Axes]** – always display both Axis for all combo charts
9. **[X and Y-Axis Title]** – display at least Y-Axis title for dual Axis configuration so the audience can quickly identify metrics displayed on both sides.
10. **[Background]** – this is gray in the above Scorecard, but the default will depend on how you have set up your theme.
11. **[Border Radius]** – 4 in this example
12. **[Border Color]** – this is transparent in this chart, but the default will depend on how you have set up your theme.
13. **[Border Shadow]** – applied in the above charts. The default is not selected
14. **[Legend]** – best practice to display the legends if your chart has more than one metric.

Other Configurations: Left To Default

15. **[Series Number Format]** – individual series (selected metrics of your chart) can be displayed as Cumulative or Compact Numbers with a decimal precision
16. **[Line Smooth]** – unselected
17. **[Reference Line]** – none, max ten reference lines are allowed. Please refer to page 13 for a detailed explanation.
18. **[Reverse X and Y-Axis]** – individually or both Axis can be reversed. If we reverse the X-Axis for the above chart, Saturday will show first instead of Sunday
19. **[Axis Min & Max Value and Custom Interval]** – leave this to default auto and will adjust the bar height automatically based on the metric value.
20. **[Log Scale]** – Log scales are automatically defined based on the Metrics value and will change both Left Y-Axis and Pub/bar size
21. **[Grid Configuration]** – consists of Axis Color, Grid Color, Font Family, Font Size, Label Font Size, Chart Backboard, and Border color.
22. **[Background and Border]** – customizable; please refer to page 8 for a detailed explanation.
23. **[Legend]** – the default position is top. Other options are left, bottom, top, and none. Please refer to page 13 for a detailed explanation.
24. **[Chart Header]** – please refer to page 12 for a detailed explanation.

Recommended: Yes

- A Double Axis configuration works well If one of the metrics you are comparing is significantly smaller than the rest of the set.
- Unless X-Axis is a date, keep the number of pubs/bars to a max of 15.

Chapter 9: Table

Tables represent quantitative information where precise values can be required in some cases. However, this is not exclusive in this information age. My personal favorite method of using tables treats them as a raw data export into Microsoft Excel and Google Sheets for detailed analysis.

Use case:

1. **Table:** Tables can handle large data sets, and in many cases, Tables are the most suitable for displaying a large data set. Please use the chart type that best suits your need.
2. **Table with bars:** The "Table with bars" is very similar to the "Table chart" except that the "Table with bars" has the option to display the value as horizontal bars. It's possible to display both Bars and Bars with Numbers.
3. **Table with heatmap:** A "Table with heatmap" is also similar to the "Table chart" except for the heatmap, which adds additional visual comparison where the highest value will have the highest color contrast.

Recommended: Yes

Please use the chart type that best suits your need.

Table Chart in Google Data Studio			
Chart Type	Grand total	Comparison	Recommended
Table	Always	Yes, if data set allows	Yes
Table with bars	Always	Yes, if data set allows	Yes
Table with heatmap	Always	Yes, if data set allows	Yes (Personal fav)

Recommended Configurations For Table:

1. **[Table Title]** – title is not necessary. Personally, I always prefer to have a title for each chart.
2. **[Table Header]** – shown as default and best practice to Display header.
3. **[Grand Total]** – add "Grand total" by selecting "Show summary row" in the DATA tab for all tables so you can compare against an individual table element
4. **[Row Numbers]** – especially, if all the rows are not visible in the table, display the row number so the audience can see there is more data hidden in the table

5. **[Pagination]** – hidden data in the Table can be scrolled down, but Pagination provides easy navigation and is an additional option to see hidden data. It's best practice to display Pagination if you have 100s rows of data.
6. **[Comparison]** – "% Change" (optional) in the above table. If your data set allows, its best practice to display comparison metrics for a table.
7. **[Show Compare and Absolute Change]** – individually for each metric
8. **[Horizontal scrolling]** – if all the dimensions are not visible in the table make sure to select the "Horizontal scrolling".

Others Configurations Available Within Table Charts:

9. **[Conditional Formatting]** – please refer to page 10 for a detailed explanation.
10. **[Table Header]** – consist of "Show header", "Wrap text", Font Color, Size, and Font Family. If table Body doesn't fit in a column, you can use Wrap Text
11. **[Table Color]** – consist of Header background color, Cell border color, Odd row color, Even row color, Positive and Negative Change Color.
12. **[Positive and Negative Change Color]** – you can also customize the color for the increase and decrease; for example, you may want to display a decrease in green for Bounce Rate or Negative Sentiment
13. **[Table Labels]** – consist of Font Color, Size, and Font Family
14. **[Table Body]** – consist of Row numbers, Wrap text, and Horizontal scrolling.
15. **[Table Footer]** – consist of "Show page navigation", "Compact page navigation", Footer border color, Footer border weight, and Footer border style. Default is selected none.
16. **[Missing Data]** – options include "null", 0, - ("-"), No data, and Blank (""). Please refer to page 9 for a detailed explanation.
17. **[Dimension and Metric Column]** – individually aligned to left, middle, or right. Default aligned left for Dimension and Metrics on the right
18. **[Metrics Number Format and Decimal Precision]** – individually for a metric.
19. **[Background and Border]** – customizable; please refer to page 8 for a detailed explanation.
20. **[Legend]** – the default position is top. Other options are left, bottom, top, and none. Please refer to page 13 for a detailed explanation.
21. **[Chart Header]** – chart headers allow viewers to perform several actions on charts, such as data export, drilling up or down, and view charts in explorer tools. Please refer to page 12 for a detailed explanation.

I. Table

Tables represent quantitative information where precise values can be required in some cases. However, this is not exclusive in this information age. My personal favorite method of using tables treats them as a raw data export into Microsoft Excel and Google Sheets for detailed analysis (last example).

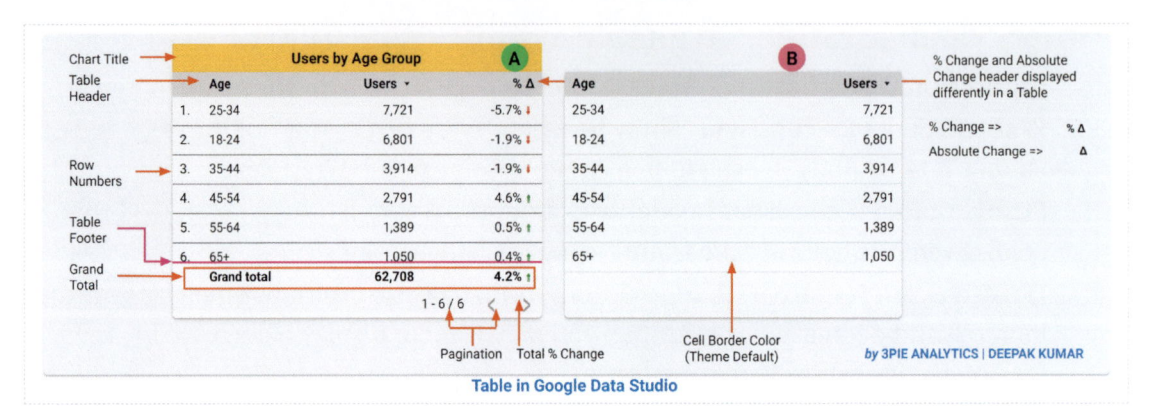

Table in Google Data Studio

— In this chart, we are displaying Users by Age Group and comparing them with previous time periods.

Chart Configurations:

1. **[Table Title]** – in a table, you have the option to display the Table header, and the title is not necessary. Personally, I always prefer to have a title for each chart.
2. **[Table Header]** – shown as default and best practice to Display header. You can also customize the Font Color, Font Size, and Font Family.
3. **[Row Numbers]** – we only have six rows of the data but If all the rows are not visible in the table, display the row number so the audience can see there is more data hidden in the table
4. **[Grand Total]** – add "Grand total" by selecting "Show summary row" in the DATA tab for all tables so you can compare against an individual table element
5. **[Pagination]** – hidden data in the Table can be scrolled down, but Pagination provides easy navigation and is an additional option to see hidden data. It's best practice to display Pagination if you have 100s rows of data.
6. **[Comparison]** – "% Change" (optional) in the above table. If your data allows, its best practice to display comparison metrics for a table.
7. **[Horizontal scrolling]** – if all the dimensions are not visible in the table make sure to select the "Horizontal scrolling".

Other Configurations: Left To Default

8. **[Conditional Formatting]** – please refer to page 10 for a detailed explanation.
9. **[Table Header]** – consist of "Show header", "Wrap text", Font Color, Size, and Font Family. If table Body doesn't fit in a column, you can use Wrap Text
10. **[Table Color]** – consist of Header background color, Cell border color, Odd row color, Even row color, Positive and Negative Change Color.
11. **[Positive and Negative Change Color]** – you can also customize the color for the increase and decrease; for example, you may want to display a decrease in green for Bounce Rate or Negative Sentiment
12. **[Table Labels]** – consist of Font Color, Size, and Font Family
13. **[Table Body]** – consist of Row numbers, Wrap text, and Horizontal scrolling.
14. **[Table Footer]** – consist of "Show page navigation", "Compact page navigation", Footer border color, Footer border weight, and Footer border style. Default is selected none.
15. **[Missing Data]** – options include "null", 0, - ("-"), No data, and Blank (""). Please refer to page 9 for a detailed explanation.
16. **[Dimension and Metric Column]** – individually aligned to left, middle, or right. Default aligned left for Dimension and Metrics on the right
17. **[Metrics Number Format and Decimal Precision]** – individually for a metric.
18. **[Background and Border]** – customizable; please refer to page 8 for a detailed explanation.
19. **[Legend]** – the default position is top. Other options are left, bottom, top, and none. Please refer to page 13 for a detailed explanation.
20. **[Chart Header]** – chart headers allow viewers to perform several actions on charts, such as data export, drilling up or down, and view charts in explorer tools. Please refer to page 12 for a detailed explanation.

Recommended: Yes [Table A]

- Both Tables and Pivot Tables can handle large data sets, and in many cases these two charts are the most suitable for displaying a large data set. Please use the chart type that best suits your need.

II. Table with bars

The "Table with bars" is very similar to the "Table chart" except that the "Table with bars" has the option to display the value as horizontal bars. It's possible to display both Bars and Bars with Numbers. In the table with bars you can also set target for each metric

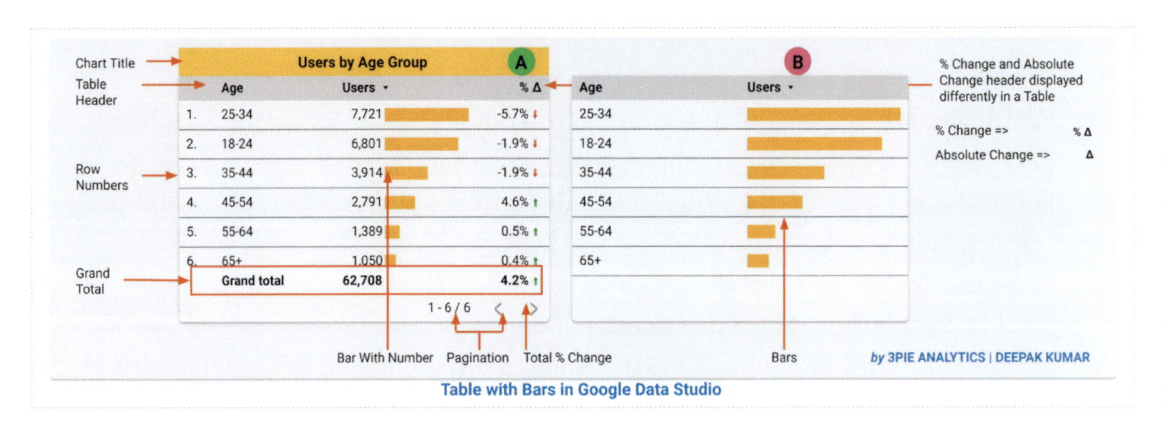

Table with Bars in Google Data Studio

– In this chart, we are displaying Users by Age Group

Chart Configurations:

1. **[Table Title]** – title is not necessary. Personally, I always prefer to have a title for each chart.
2. **[Table Header]** – shown as default and best practice to Display header.
3. **[Row Numbers]** – we only have six rows of the data but If all the rows are not visible in the table, display the row number so the audience can see there is more data hidden in the table
4. **[Grand Total]** – add "Grand total" by selecting "Show summary row" in the DATA tab for all tables so you can compare against an individual table element
5. **[Pagination]** – hidden data in the Table can be scrolled down, but Pagination provides easy navigation and is an additional option to see hidden data. It's best practice to display Pagination if you have 100s rows of data.
6. **[Comparison]** – "% Change" (optional) in the above table. If your data allows, its best practice to display comparison metrics for a table.
7. **["Grand total" and " Total % Change"]** – if you have configured your chart to display comparison, select the "Show summary row" option in the DATA tab, which will display the "Grand total" for the table.
8. **[Horizontal scrolling]** – if all the dimensions are not visible in the table make sure to select the "Horizontal scrolling".

Other Configurations: Left To Default

9. **[Conditional Formatting]** – please refer to page 10 for a detailed explanation.
10. **[Table Header]** – consist of "Show header", "Wrap text", Font Color, Size, and Font Family. If table Body doesn't fit in a column, you can use Wrap Text
11. **[Table Color]** – consist of Header background color, Cell border color, Odd row color, Even row color, Positive and Negative Change Color.
12. **[Positive and Negative Change Color]** – you can also customize the color for the increase and decrease; for example, you may want to display a decrease in green for Bounce Rate or Negative Sentiment
13. **[Table Labels]** – consist of Font Color, Size, and Font Family
14. **[Table Body]** – consist of Row numbers, Wrap text, and Horizontal scrolling.
15. **[Table Footer]** – consist of "Show page navigation", "Compact page navigation", Footer border color, Footer border weight, and Footer border style. Default is selected none.
16. **[Show target and color]** – with an option to put a single value/raw number for each metrics. Color can be configured as well
17. **[Show axis]** – axis font color and family and Axis compact numbers
18. **[Bar/Pub]** – if you selected the Bar/Pub in the previous step you will option including, Show numbers with Compact number and Decimal precision configuration, Show target with an option to put a single value/raw number for each metrics, Show Axis with Font color and Family and Axis compact number configuration, Show compare, and Show absolute change
19. **[Missing Data]** – options include "null", 0, - ("-"), No data, and Blank (""). Please refer to page 9 for a detailed explanation.
20. **[Dimension and Metric Column]** – individually aligned to left, middle, or right. Default aligned left for Dimension and Metrics on the right
21. **[Metrics Number Format and Decimal Precision]** – individually for a metric.
22. **[Background and Border]** – customizable; please refer to page 8 for a detailed explanation.
23. **[Legend]** – the default position is top. Other options are left, bottom, top, and none. Please refer to page 13 for a detailed explanation.
24. **[Chart Header]** – chart headers allow viewers to perform several actions on charts, such as data export, drilling up or down, and view charts in explorer tools. Please refer to page 12 for a detailed explanation.

Recommended: Yes [Table A]

- The "Table with bars" is very similar to the "Table chart" except that the "Table with bars" has the option to display the value as horizontal bars. It's possible to display both Bars and Bars with Numbers.

III. Table with Heatmap

A "Table with heatmap" is also similar to the "Table chart" except for the heatmap, which adds additional visual comparison where the highest value will have the highest color contrast.

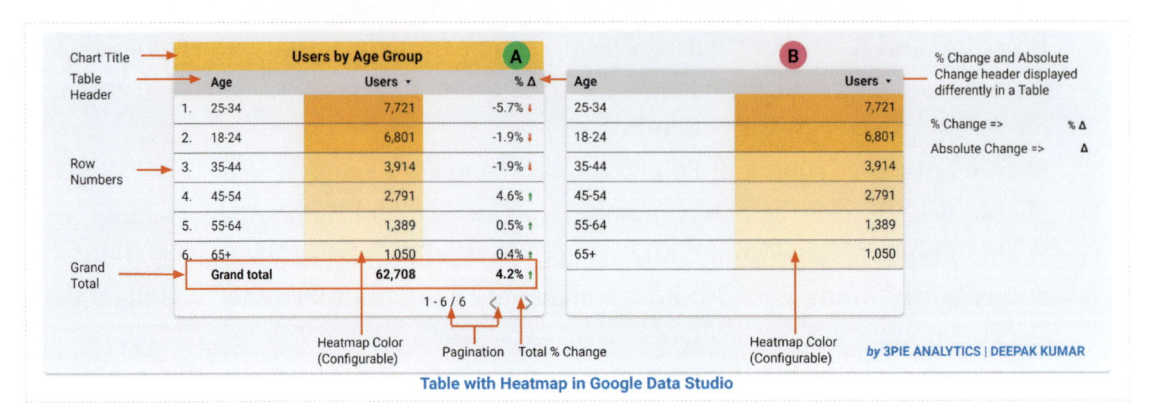

Table with Heatmap in Google Data Studio

— In this chart, we are displaying Users by Age Group

Chart Configurations:

1. **[Heatmap Color]** – a Table is designed to represent quantitative information where precise values are required. The Heatmap adds an additional visual comparison.
2. **[Table Title]** – in a table, you have the option to display the Table header, and the title is not necessary. Personally, I always prefer to have a title for each chart.
3. **[Table Header]** – shown as default and best practice to Display header. You can also customize the Font Color, Font Size, and Font Family.
4. **[Row Numbers]** – we only have six rows of the data but If all the rows are not visible in the table, display the row number so the audience can see there is more data hidden in the table
5. **[Grand Total]** – add "Grand total" by selecting "Show summary row" in the DATA tab for all tables so you can compare against an individual table element
6. **[Pagination]** – hidden data in the Table can be scrolled down, but Pagination provides easy navigation and is an additional option to see hidden data. It's best practice to display Pagination if you have 100s rows of data.
7. **[Comparison]** – "% Change" (optional) in the above table. If your data allows, its best practice to display comparison metrics for a table.
8. **["Grand total" and " Total % Change"]** – if you have configured your chart to display comparison, select the "Show summary row" option in the DATA tab, which will display the "Grand total" for the table.
9. **[Horizontal scrolling]** – if all the dimensions are not visible in the table make sure to select the "Horizontal scrolling".

Page 94

Other Configurations: Left To Default

10. **[Conditional Formatting]** – you can also add Conditional formatting in a Table Chart. Please refer to page 10 for a detailed explanation.
11. **[Table Header]** – consist of "Show header", "Wrap text", Font Color, Size, and Font Family. If table Body doesn't fit in a column, you can use Wrap Text
12. **[Table Color]** – consist of Header background color, Cell border color, Odd row color, Even row color, Positive and Negative Change Color.
13. **[Positive and Negative Change Color]** – you can also customize the color for the increase and decrease; for example, you may want to display a decrease in green for Bounce Rate or Negative Sentiment
14. **[Table Labels]** – consist of Font Color, Size, and Font Family
15. **[Table Body]** – consist of Row numbers, Wrap text, and Horizontal scrolling.
16. **[Table Footer]** – consist of "Show page navigation", "Compact page navigation", Footer border color, Footer border weight, and Footer border style. Default is selected none.
17. **[Missing Data]** – options include "null", 0, - ("-"), No data, and Blank (""). Please refer to page 9 for a detailed explanation.
18. **[Dimension and Metric Column]** – individually aligned to left, middle, or right. Default aligned left for Dimension and Metrics on the right
19. **[Metrics Number Format and Decimal Precision]** – individually for a metric.
20. **[Background and Border]** – customizable; please refer to page 8 for a detailed explanation.
21. **[Legend]** – the default position is top. Other options are left, bottom, top, and none. Please refer to page 13 for a detailed explanation.
22. **[Chart Header]** – chart headers allow viewers to perform several actions on charts, such as data export, drilling up or down, and view charts in explorer tools. Please refer to page 12 for a detailed explanation.

Recommended: Yes [Table A]

- A "Table with heatmap" is also similar to the "Table chart" except for the heatmap, which adds additional visual comparison where the highest value will have the highest color contrast.

IV. RAW Data Table

A personal favorite, a RAW table can handle and display large sets of data. Treat tables as raw data for export into Excel/Google Sheets for a custom chart or detailed analysis.

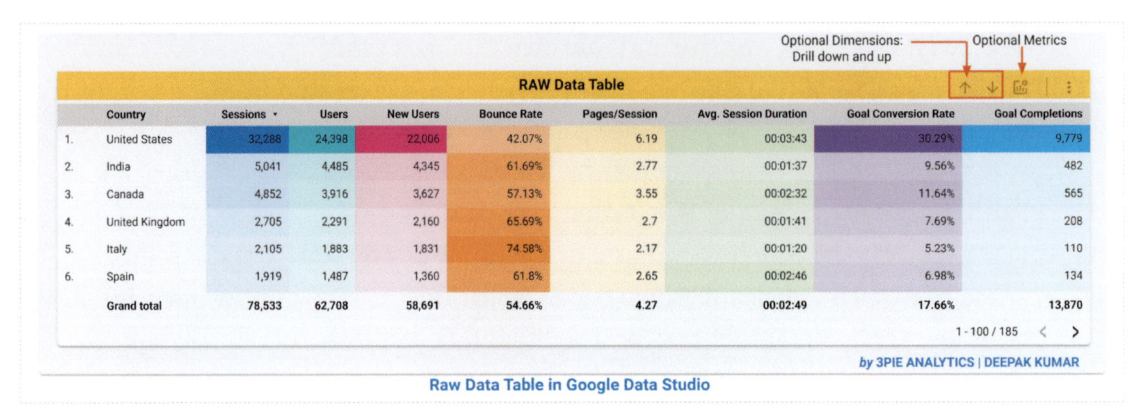

Raw Data Table in Google Data Studio

- RAW data table which consists of all the reporting metrics and dimensions of the report.

Chart Configurations:

1. **[Optional Dimension & Metrics]** – these are configurable in the DATA tab. Select the "Drill down" checkbox for Dimensions and "Optional metrics" for Metrics. You can extract/visualize the data with a combination of metrics and dimensions, including the optional.
2. **[Optional Dimension: Drill up and down]** – in a table, you can also add optional dimensions, for example Date, Month, City, and Channels. Once you drill up or down (depending on the setup), you can change from County to any optional dimension you have set.
3. **[Optional Metrics]** – these work in the same way as optional dimensions. If it's not possible to fit all the metrics in your Table, use Optional metrics.

Recommended: Yes, A Personal Favorite

- For raw data for export into Excel/Google Sheets for a custom chart or details analysis

Other useful Configurations for a table:

Adjust Column Size

To manually resize individual columns in the table, click the column divider and drag it to where you want it. To resize multiple columns at once, hold the Shift key while dragging a column divider.

Drill Down:

Drilling down gives viewers a way to reveal additional levels of detail within a chart. This option appears on charts that support drill down. When you turn on Drill down, each dimension you add becomes another level of detail you can drill into. When drill-down is enabled on a chart, you can for example:
- Drill down from a higher level of detail to a lower one (e.g., from Country to City).
- Drill up from a lower level of detail to a higher one (e.g., from City to Country).

Optional Metrics:

Define a list of additional metrics in the DATA tab that can be displayed by the chart or table.

Sort Your Data:

Report viewers can sort the data by clicking on a column header. Each click reverses the sort order: e.g., click once to sort in ascending (lowest to highest) order, click again to sort in descending (highest to lowest) order.

Rows Per Page:

Use the Rows per page option to control how many table rows to display per table page. Show pagination must be selected for this to take effect.

Show Summary Row:

The Show summary row at the bottom of a table summarizes each metric column
- **Table Colors:** These options control the colors of the table borders and cells.
- **Header background color:** Sets the color of the table header background.
- **Cell border color:** Sets the color of the border between rows.
- **Odd/Even row color:** Sets the color of odd or even rows in the table.

Tables Limitations:

The number of dimensions and metrics you can add depends on the data source selected in the table:
- Tables based on "fixed schema" data sources, such as Google Analytics and Google Ads can have up to 10 dimensions and 20 metrics.
- Tables based on "flexible schema" data sources, such as Google Sheets, BigQuery, and SQL can have up to 100 dimensions and 100 metrics.

Chapter 10: Pivot Tables

A Pivot Table stores the summary of a specific data set in a condensed manner or groups data together in a meaningful way. My personal favorite method is to treat Pivot Tables as a raw data export into Excel and Google Sheets for detailed analysis.

Use case:

1. **Pivot Table:** Pivot Tables can handle large data sets, and, in most cases, Pivot charts are the most suitable choice for displaying and summarizing an extensive data set.
2. **Pivot Table with bars:** The "Pivot Table with bars" is very similar to the "Pivot Table" except that the "Pivot Table with bars" has the option to display the value as horizontal bars. It's possible to display both Bars and Bars with Numbers.
3. **Pivot Table with heatmap:** A "Pivot Table with heatmap" is also similar to the "Pivot Table chart" except for the heatmap, which adds additional visual comparison where the highest value will have the highest color contrast.

Recommended: Yes, see the chart version that suits your need

Pivot Table in Google Data Studio			
Chart Type	Grand total	Comparison	Recommended
Pivot Table	Always	Yes, if data set allows	Yes
Pivot Table with bar	Always	Yes, if data set allows	Yes
Pivot Table with heatmap	Always	Yes, if data set allows	Yes, personal favorite

Pivot Table Limitation:

1. **[Column Dimension]** – max 2 Column Dimensions are allowed
2. **[Row Dimension]** – max 5 Row Dimensions are allowed
3. **[Number of Pivot Table on a Page/Slide]** – max 5 Pivot Tables are allowed on each page/slide
4. **[Number of Metrics]** – up to 10

Table Configurations Not Available Inside Pivot Table

5. **[Comparison]**

6. **[Row Numbers]**
7. **[Pagination]**
8. **[Table Footer]**
9. **[Dimension and Metric Column alignment]**

Recommended Configurations For Pivot Tables:

10. **[Table Title]** – title is not necessary. Personally, I always prefer to have a title for each chart.
11. **[Table Header]** – default and not possible to hide
12. **[Grand Total]** – add "Grand total" for both Row and Column for all tables so you can compare against an individual table element
13. **[Subtotal]** – if you have more than one Dimension/Metrics, Subtotal can be configured in the DATA tab
14. **[Expand – collapse]** – it's recommended that this is avoided – even after working in the Data Analytics field for over eight years, I still find this confusing! However, if you do choose to use it, this operates similarly to Optional Dimensions for other charts, though there is no way to deselect the default dimension. Last example in this chapter.
15. **[Metrics # Format and Decimal Precision]** – individually for metrics. Default show as a raw number with 0 Decimal precision
16. **[Conditional Formatting]** – you can also add Conditional formatting in a Pivot Table. Please refer to page 10 for a detailed explanation.

Others Configurations Available Within Pivot Table:

17. **[Table Header and Label]** – consist of Font Color, Size, and Font Family
18. **[Table Color]** – header background color, Cell border color, Highlighted color, Odd row color, and Even row color.
19. **[Missing Data]** – left to default and will show "-" other options includes Show "No data", Show "0", show "null", and show "" (blank). Please refer to page 9 for a detailed explanation.
20. **[Metrics # Format and Decimal Precision]** – individually for metrics. Default show as a raw number with 0 Decimal precision.
21. **[Metrics #]** – here you can individually configure to display as "Bar/Pub", "Number" or "Heatmap" for each metric.
22. **[Background and Border]** – customizable; please refer to page 8 for a detailed explanation.
23. **[Legend]** – the default position is top. Other options are left, bottom, top, and none. Please refer to page 13 for a detailed explanation.
24. **[Chart Header]** – please refer to page 12 for a detailed explanation.

I. Pivot Table

A Pivot Table stores the summary of a specific data set in a condensed manner or groups data together in a meaningful way. My personal favorite method is to treat Pivot Tables as a raw data export into Excel and Google Sheets for detailed analysis.

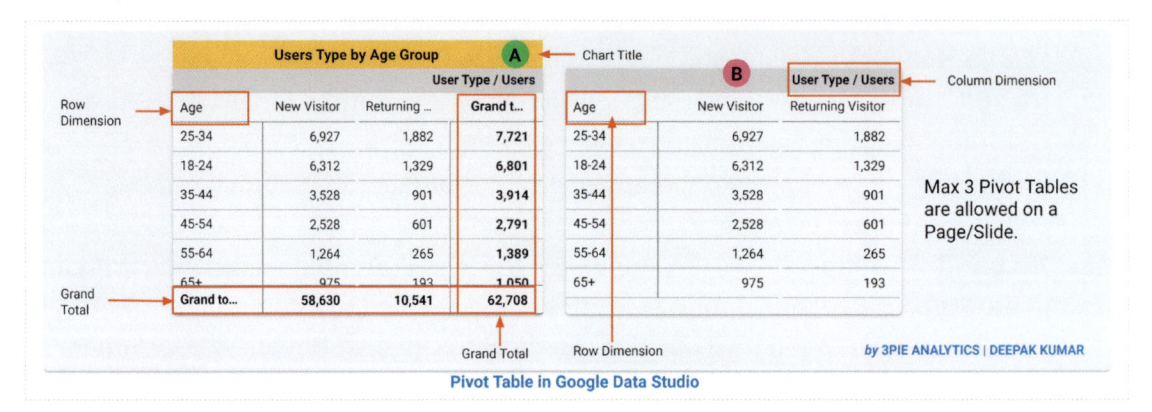

Pivot Table in Google Data Studio

- In this chart we are displaying Users by Age Group and Users Type for the selected time range.

Pivot Table Limitation:
1. **[Column Dimension]** – max 2 Column Dimensions are allowed
2. **[Row Dimension]** – max 5 Row Dimensions are allowed
3. **[Number of Pivot Table on a Page/Slide]** – max 5 Pivot Tables are allowed on each page/slide
4. **[Number of Metrics]** – up to 10

Chart Configurations:
1. **[Table Title]** – title is not necessary. Personally, I always prefer to have a title for each chart.
2. **[Table Header]** – default and not possible to hide
3. **[Grand Total]** – add "Grand total" for both Row and Column for all tables so you can compare against an individual table element
4. **[Subtotal]** – if you have more than one Dimension/Metrics, Subtotal can be configured in the DATA tab
5. **[Expand – collapse]** – it's recommended that this is avoided - even after working in the Data Analytics field for over eight years, I still find this confusing! However, if you do choose to use it, this operates similarly to Optional Dimensions for other charts, though there is no way to deselect the default dimension. Last example in this chapter.

6. **[Background]** – this is gray in the above Scorecard, but the default will depend on how you have set up your theme.
7. **[Border Radius]** – 4 in this example
8. **[Border Color]** – this is transparent in this chart, but the default will depend on how you have set up your theme.
9. **[Border Shadow]** – applied in the above charts. The default is not selected

Other Configurations: Left To Default

10. **[Conditional Formatting]** – you can also add Conditional formatting in a Pivot Table. Please refer to page 10 for a detailed explanation.
11. **[Table Header and Label]** – consist of Font Color, Size, and Font Family
12. **[Table Color]** – header background color, Cell border color, Highlighted color, Odd row color, and Even row color.
13. **[Missing Data]** – left to default and will show "-" other options includes Show "No data", Show "0", show "null", and show "" (blank). Please refer to page 9 for a detailed explanation.
14. **[Metrics # Format and Decimal Precision]** – individually for metrics. Default show as a raw number with 0 Decimal precision.
15. **[Metrics #]** – here you can individually configure to display as "Bar/Pub", "Number" or "Heat map" for each metric. If you have selected option "Show numbers" default will show as a raw number with "0" Decimal precision which can be configured accordingly.
16. **[Background Color, Border Radius, and Opacity]** – customizable; please refer to page 8 for a detailed explanation.
17. **[Border Color, Weight, and Style]** – customizable; please refer to page 8 for a detailed explanation.
18. **[Chart Header]** – chart headers allow viewers to perform several actions on charts, such as data export, drilling up or down, and view charts in explorer tools. Please refer to page 12 for a detailed explanation.

Recommended: Yes [Table A]

- Both Pivot Tables and Tables can handle large data sets and in most cases these two types of charts are the most suitable choice for displaying an extensive data set.

II. Pivot Table With Bars

A pivot table stores the summary of a specific data set in a condensed manner or groups data sets together in a meaningful way. My personal favorite method is to treat Pivot Tables as a raw data export into Excel and Google Sheets for detailed analysis.

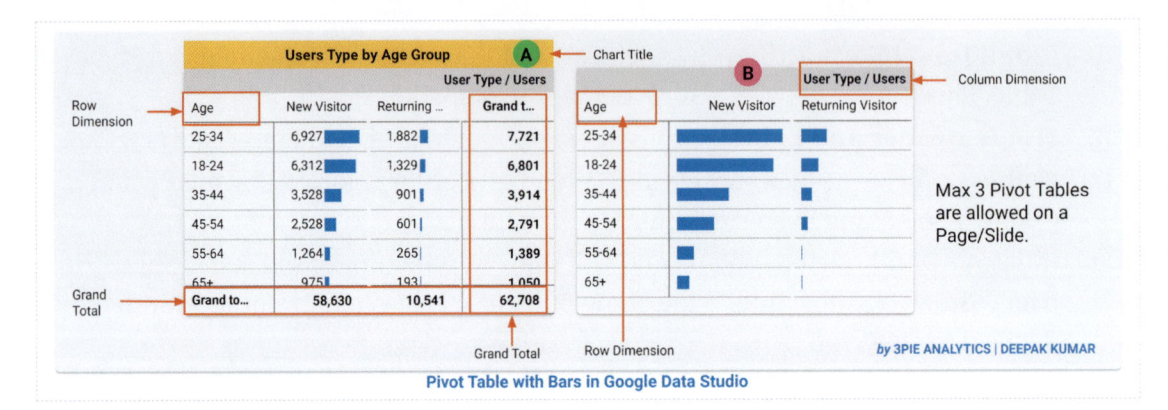

Pivot Table with Bars in Google Data Studio

- In this chart we are displaying Users by Age Group and Users Type for the selected time range.

Pivot Table Limitation:

1. **[Column Dimension]** – max 2 Column Dimensions are allowed
2. **[Row Dimension]** – max 5 Row Dimensions are allowed
3. **[Number of Pivot Table on a Page/Slide]** – max 5 Pivot Tables are allowed on each page/slide
4. **[Number of Metrics]** – up to 10

Chart Configurations:

5. **[Table Title]** – title is not necessary. Personally, I always prefer to have a title for each chart.
6. **[Table Header]** – default and not possible to hide
7. **[Grand Total]** – add "Grand total" for both Row and Column for all tables so you can compare against an individual table element
8. **[Subtotal]** – if you have more than one Dimension/Metrics, Subtotal can be configured in the DATA tab
9. **[Expand – collapse]** – it's recommended that this is avoided – even after working in the Data Analytics field for over eight years, I still find this confusing! However, if you do choose to use it, this operates similarly to Optional Dimensions for other charts, though there is no way to deselect the default dimension. Last example in this chapter.

10. **[Pub/bar Data label]** – default unselected, if both number and Pub fits nicely, display the data labels as well
11. **[Background]** – this is gray in the above Scorecard, but the default will depend on how you have set up your theme.
12. **[Border Radius]** – 4 in this example
13. **[Border Color]** – this is transparent in this chart, but the default will depend on how you have set up your theme.
14. **[Border Shadow]** – applied in the above charts. The default is not selected

Other Configurations: Left To Default

15. **[Conditional Formatting]** – you can also add Conditional formatting in a Pivot Table. Please refer to page 10 for a detailed explanation.
16. **[Table Header and Label]** – consist of Font Color, Size, and Font Family
17. **[Table Color]** – header background color, Cell border color, Highlighted color, Odd row color, and Even row color.
18. **[Missing Data]** – left to default and will show "-" other options includes Show "No data", Show "0", show "null", and show "" (blank). Please refer to page 9 for a detailed explanation.
19. **[Metrics #]** – here you can individually configure to display as "Bar/Pub", "Number" or "Heatmap" for each metric. If you have selected option "Pub/bar" you can assign a custom color
20. **[Pub/bar Color]** – customizable; you can assign a custom color
21. **["Show numbers" with Compact numbers configuration]** – to display both numbers and Pub
22. **[Bar Scaling]** – default set to "Relative to data Range" and can be switch to "Start at 0."
23. **[Background Color, Border Radius, and Opacity]** – customizable; please refer to page 8 for a detailed explanation.
24. **[Border Color, Weight, and Style]** – customizable; please refer to page 8 for a detailed explanation.
25. **[Chart Header]** – chart headers allow viewers to perform several actions on charts, such as data export, drilling up or down, and view charts in explorer tools. Please refer to page 12 for a detailed explanation.

Recommended: Yes [Table A]

- Both Pivot Tables and Tables can handle large data sets and in most cases these two types of charts are the most suitable choice for displaying an extensive data set.

III. Pivot Table With Heatmap

A pivot table stores the summary of a specific data set in a condensed manner or groups data sets together in a meaningful way. My personal favorite method is to treat Pivot Tables as a raw data export into Excel and Google Sheets for detailed analysis.

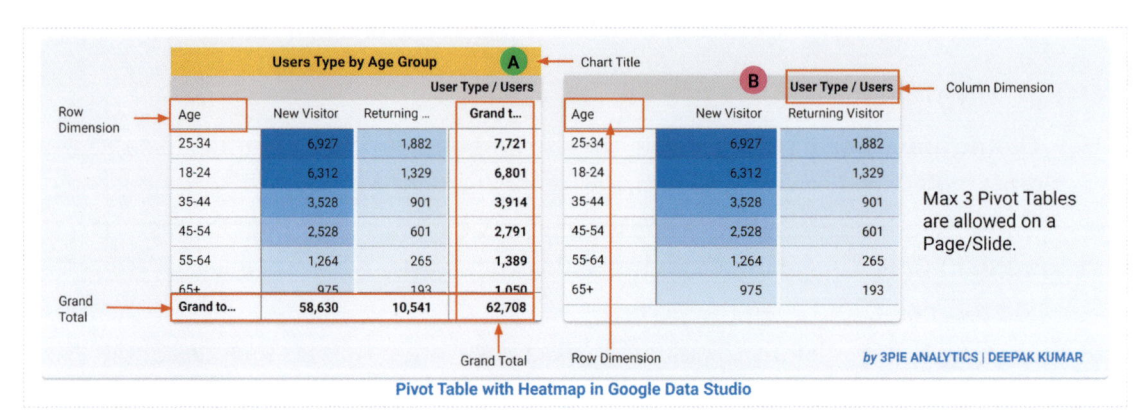

Pivot Table with Heatmap in Google Data Studio

– In this chart we are displaying Users by Age Group and Users Type for the selected time range.

Pivot Table Limitation:

1. **[Column Dimension]** – max 2 Column Dimensions are allowed
2. **[Row Dimension]** – Max 5 Row Dimensions are allowed
3. **[Number of Pivot Table on a Page/Slide]** – Max 5 Pivot Tables are allowed on each page/slide
4. **[Number of Metrics]** – Up to 10

Chart Configurations:

1. **[Heat Map Color]** – configurable and Heatmap color can be configured in the STYLE tab
2. **[Table Title]** – title is not necessary. Personally, I always prefer to have a title for each chart.
3. **[Table Header]** – default and not possible to hide
4. **[Grand Total]** – add "Grand total" for both Row and Column for all tables so you can compare against an individual table element
5. **[Subtotal]** – if you have more than one Dimension/Metrics, Subtotal can be configured in the DATA tab

Page 104

6. **[Expand – collapse]** – it's recommended that this is avoided – even after working in the Data Analytics field for over eight years, I still find this confusing! However, if you do choose to use it, this operates similarly to Optional Dimensions for other charts, though there is no way to deselect the default dimension. An example is shown below.
7. **[Background]** – this is gray in the above Scorecard, but the default will depend on how you have set up your theme.
8. **[Border Radius]** – 4 in this example
9. **[Border Color]** – this is transparent in this chart, but the default will depend on how you have set up your theme.
10. **[Border Shadow]** – applied in the above charts. The default is not selected

Other Configurations: Left To Default

11. **[Conditional Formatting]** – you can also add Conditional formatting in a Pivot Table. Please refer to page 10 for a detailed explanation.
12. **[Table Header and Label]** – consist of Font Color, Size, and Font Family
13. **[Heatmap Text Contrast]** – leave to default None, unless you make a report for a specific audience. Options are Low, Medium, and High.
14. **[Table Color]** – header background color, Cell border color, Highlighted color, Odd row color, and Even row color.
15. **[Missing Data]** – left to default and will show "-" other options includes Show "No data", Show "0", show "null", and show "" (blank). Please refer to page 9 for a detailed explanation.
16. **[Metrics # Format and Decimal Precision]** – individually for metrics. Default show as a raw number with 0 Decimal precision.
17. **[Metrics #]** – here you can individually configure to display as "Bar/Pub", "Number" or "Heatmap" for each metric. If you have selected option "Heatmap" you can assign a custom color
18. **[Background Color, Border Radius, and Opacity]** – customizable; please refer to page 8 for a detailed explanation.
19. **[Border Color, Weight, and Style]** – customizable; please refer to page 8 for a detailed explanation.
20. **[Chart Header]** – chart headers allow viewers to perform several actions on charts, such as data export, drilling up or down, and view charts in explorer tools. Please refer to page 12 for a detailed explanation.

Recommended: Yes [Table A]

– Both Pivot Tables and Tables can handle large data sets and in most cases these two types of charts are the most suitable choice for displaying an extensive data set.

IV. Pivot Table With Bars: with "Expand – collapse" option

"Default expands level." Is fixed and not possible to deselect (country in the below example). Secondary expand level can be selected or deselect (Continent and Sub-Continent in the below example)

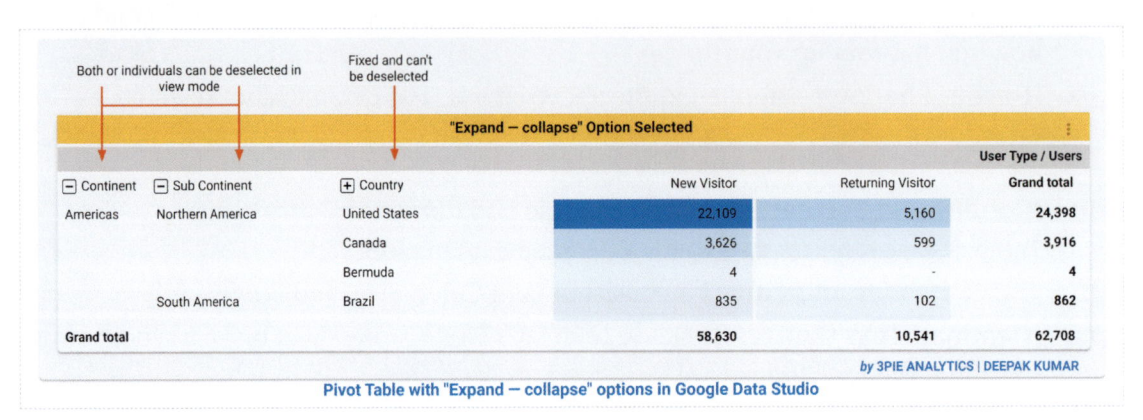

			New Visitor	Returning Visitor	Grand total
Continent	Sub Continent	Country			User Type / Users
Americas	Northern America	United States	22,109	5,160	24,398
		Canada	3,626	599	3,916
		Bermuda	4	-	4
	South America	Brazil	835	102	862
Grand total			58,630	10,541	62,708

Both or individuals can be deselected in view mode | *Fixed and can't be deselected*

"Expand — collapse" Option Selected

by 3PIE ANALYTICS | DEEPAK KUMAR

Pivot Table with "Expand — collapse" options in Google Data Studio

- **[Expand – collapse]** – it's recommended that this is avoided – even after working in the Data Analytics field for over eight years, I still find this confusing! However, if you do choose to use it, this operates similarly to Optional Dimensions for other charts, though there is no way to deselect the default dimension. An example is shown below.

Recommended: No

- Hard to digest the data and structure for most of the users. Please avoid "Expand – collapse" in a Pivot Table

Others Pivot Table Limitations:

1. **[Max 50,000 rows of Data]** – up to 50,000 rows of data can be processed in pivot tables. However, depending on the dataset and the dimensions and metrics in the table, table data may load slow. You can apply a filter to reduce the amount of data processed.
2. **[Number of Dimensions]** – the number of row dimensions available depends on the type of data you are connecting to:
   a. Tables based on "fixed schema" data sources, such as Google Analytics and Google Ads can have up to 10 dimensions and 20 metrics.
   b. Tables based on "flexible schema" data sources, such as Google Sheets, BigQuery, and SQL can have up to 100 dimensions and 100 metrics.
3. **[Column Dimension]** – max 2 Column Dimensions are allowed
4. **[Row Dimension]** – max 5 Row Dimensions are allowed
5. **[Number of Pivot Table on a Page/Slide]** – max 5 Pivot Tables are allowed on each page/slide
6. **[Number of Metrics]** – up to 10

Table Configurations Not Available Inside Pivot Table:

1. **[Comparison]**
2. **[Row Numbers]**
3. **[Pagination]**
4. **[Table Footer]**
5. **[Dimension and Metric Column alignment]**
6. **[Metrics Filter]** – you will receive an error message if you apply metric filters to pivot tables because it is not supported.

Chapter 11: Area Charts

An Area Chart is best used to show the distribution of categories as parts of a whole changing over an interval. As the area inside the chart is plotted to convey whole numbers, an Area Chart does not work for negative values.

Use case:

1. **Area Chart:** to show the distribution of categories as parts of a whole changing over an interval
2. **Area Chart 100% Stacking:** if you want to split the trend over time into % share at each interval.
3. **Area Chart Show Stack:** same as Area Chart, except in this chart, the smallest series area is plotted on the top rather than bottom.

Recommended: Yes, see the chart version that suits your need

Area Chart in Google Data Studio			
Chart Type	X and Y-Axis	X and Y-Axis Title	Recommended
Area Chart	Always	Not necessary	Yes
Area Chart 100% Stacking	Always	Not necessary	Yes
Area Chart Show Stack	Always	Not necessary	No

Recommended Configurations For Area Charts:

1. **[Breakdown Dimension]** – area Chart must have a Breakdown Dimension, selected in the DATA tab.
2. **[Legend]** – always display legends for all area charts.
3. **[Chart Title]** – in an area chart, you have the option to display both Axis together with Legend, and the title is not necessary, but personally, I always prefer to have a title for each chart.
4. **[Data Label]** – not a common practice to display data labels in Area Charts
5. **[X and Y-Axis]** – always display both Axis for an area chart
6. **[X and Y-Axis Title]** – not necessary for area charts, and will save some space for both Axis, especially your chart is small
7. **[Number of Series]** – the number of series in an area chart should be kept moderate as too many series may well hinder its legibility.

Others Configurations Available Within Area Charts:

8. **[Show Stack]** – to change Area Chart to Stacked Area Chart
9. **[Show Cumulative]** – as a cumulative number
10. **[Show Points]** – add a point on each data point
11. **[Show Data Labels]** – show number at each data point
12. **[Number Format]** – compact Numbers and decimal precision. Visible if you have selected "Show Data Labels"
13. **[Color By]** – by "Series order" for unique Color for each series and "Dimension values" by single Color
14. **[Reference Line]** – none, max ten reference lines are allowed. Please refer to page 13 for a detailed explanation.
15. **[Missing Data]** – three options including Line to zero (Default Option), Line breaks, and Linear Interpolation. Please refer to page 9 for a detailed explanation.
16. **[Reverse X and Y-Axis]** – individually or both Axis can be reversed.
17. **[Axis Min and Max and Custom Interval]** – leave to default or area plotted at some point might go above the Axis.
18. **[Custom Interval for Both Axis]** – leave to default Auto. Interval controls the Axis value displayed on both Axis. 7 Interval on X-Axis will have 4 data points for a month and 12 for a year.
19. **[Log Scale]** – log scales are automatically defined based on the Metrics value and will change both Left Y-Axis and Pub/bar size
20. **[Grid Configuration]** – leave this to default. This will automatically adapt the configurations based on your chart size and color. Consists of Axis Color, Grid Color, Font Family, Font Size, Label Font Size, Chart Backboard, and Border color.
21. **[Background Color, Border Radius, and Opacity]** – customizable; please refer to page 8 for a detailed explanation.
22. **[Border Color, Weight, and Style]** – customizable; please refer to page 8 for a detailed explanation.
23. **[Legend]** – the default position is top. Other options are left, bottom, top, and none. Legend alignment (left, centre, right), Legend color, Font Family, Font Size, and Max Lines are also customizable. Please refer to page 13 for a detailed explanation.
24. **[Chart Header]** – chart headers allow viewers to perform several actions on charts, such as data export, drilling up or down, and view charts in explorer tools. Please refer to page 12 for a detailed explanation.

I. Area Chart

An Area Chart is best used to show the distribution of categories as parts of a whole changing over an interval. As the area inside the chart is plotted to convey whole numbers, an Area Chart does not work for negative values.

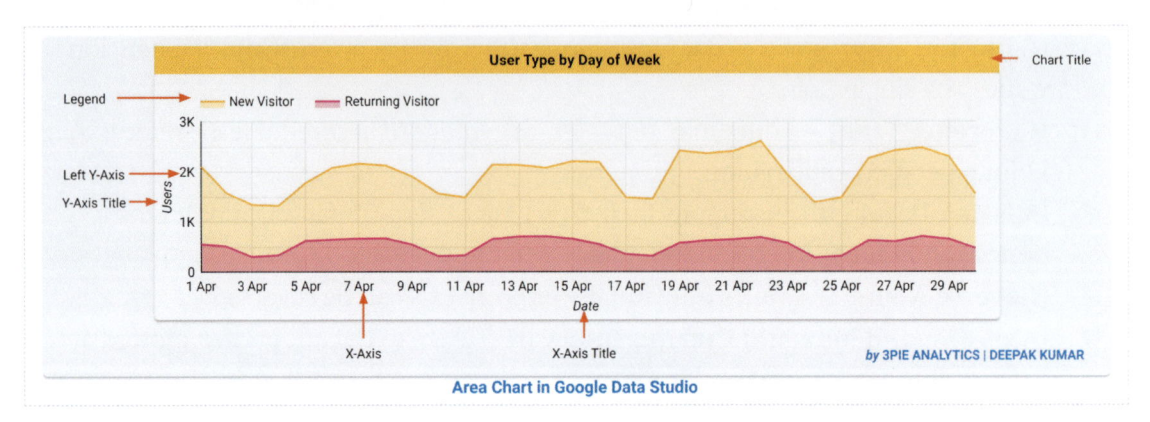

Area Chart in Google Data Studio

- In this chart, we display Users Type by weekday, and data are aggregated by weekday for the selected period.
- Left Y-Axis plotted individually on each interval, date in this example for New and Returning Visitors
- **[Breakdown Dimension]** – Area Chart must have a Breakdown Dimension, in this example, User Type

Chart Configurations:

1. **[Breakdown Dimension]** – Area Chart must have a Breakdown Dimension, selected in the DATA tab, in this example, User Type
2. **[Legend]** – always display legends if your chart has breakdown dimension, Users Type in this example
3. **[Chart Title]** – in an area chart, you have the option to display both Axis together with Legend, and the title is not necessary, but personally, I always prefer to have a title for each chart.
4. **[Data Label]** – not a common practice to display data labels in Area Charts
5. **[X and Y-Axis]** – always display both Axis for an area chart
6. **[X and Y-Axis Title]** – not necessary for area charts, and will save some space for both Axis, especially your chart is small
7. **[Number of Series]** – the number of series in an area chart should be kept moderate as too many series may well hinder its legibility.

Other Configurations: Left To Default

8. **[Show Stack]** – to change Area Chart to Stacked Area Chart
9. **[Show Cumulative]** – as a cumulative number
10. **[Show Points]** – add a point on each data point
11. **[Show Data Labels]** – show number at each data point
12. **[Number Format]** – compact Numbers and decimal precision. Visible if you have selected "Show Data Labels"
13. **[Color By]** – by "Series order" for unique Color for each series and "Dimension values" by single Color
14. **[Reference Line]** – none, max ten reference lines are allowed. Please refer to page 13 for a detailed explanation.
15. **[Missing Data]** – three options including Line to zero (Default Option), Line breaks, and Linear Interpolation. Please refer to page 9 for a detailed explanation.
16. **[Reverse X and Y-Axis]** – individually or both Axis can be reversed.
17. **[Axis Min and Max and Custom Interval]** – leave to default or area plotted at some point might go above the Axis.
18. **[Custom Interval for Both Axis]** – leave to default Auto. Interval controls the Axis value displayed on both Axis. 7 Interval on X-Axis will have 4 data points for a month and 12 for a year.
19. **[Log Scale]** – Log scales are automatically defined based on the Metrics value and will change both Left Y-Axis and Pub/bar size
20. **[Grid Configuration]** – leave this to default. This will automatically adapt the configurations based on your chart size and color. Consists of Axis Color, Grid Color, Font Family, Font Size, Label Font Size, Chart Backboard, and Border color:
21. **[Background and Border]** – customizable; please refer to page 8 for a detailed explanation.
22. **[Legend]** – the default position is top. Other options are left, bottom, top, and none. Legend alignment (left, centre, right), Legend color, Font Family, Font Size, and Max Lines are also customizable. Please refer to page 13 for a detailed explanation.
23. **[Chart Header]** – chart headers allow viewers to perform several actions on charts, such as data export, drilling up or down, and view charts in explorer tools. Please refer to page 12 for a detailed explanation.

Recommended: Yes, See The Chart Version That Suits Your Need

- **Area Chart:** to show the distribution of categories as parts of a whole changing over an interval
- **Area Chart 100% Stacking:** If you want to split the trend over time into % share at each interval.
- **Area Chart Show Stack:** Same as Area Chart, except in this chart, the smallest series area is plotted on the top rather than bottom.

II. 100% Stacked Area Chart

100% Stacked Area Chart shows the split of the categories trend over time into % share at each interval.

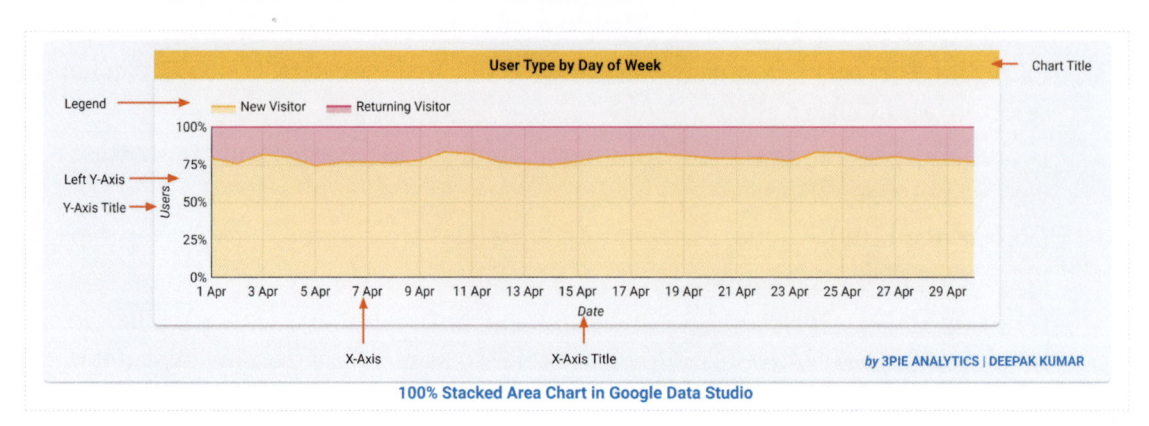

- In this chart, we display Users Type by weekday, and data are aggregated by weekday for the selected period.
- Left Y-Axis plotted individually on each interval, date in this example for New and Returning Visitors
- **[Breakdown Dimension]** – Area Chart must have a Breakdown Dimension, in this example, User Type

Chart Configurations:

1. **[Breakdown Dimension]**– area Chart must have a Breakdown Dimension, selected in the DATA tab, in this example, User Type
2. **[Legend]** – always display legends if your chart has breakdown dimension, Users Type in this example
3. **[Chart Title]** – in an area chart, you have the option to display both Axis together with Legend, and the title is not necessary, but personally, I always prefer to have a title for each chart.
4. **[Data Label]** – not a common practice to display data labels in Area Charts
5. **[X and Y-Axis]** – always display both Axis for an area chart
6. **[X and Y-Axis Title]** – not necessary for area charts, and will save some space for both Axis, especially your chart is small
7. **[Number of Series]** – the number of series in an area chart should be kept moderate as too many series may well hinder its legibility.

Other Configurations: Left To Default

8. **[Show Stack]** – deselecting this option will switch the graph to an Area Chart
9. **[Show Cumulative]** – as a cumulative number
10. **[Show Points]** – add a point on each data point

11. **[Show Data Labels]** – show number at each data point
12. **[Number Format]** – compact Numbers and decimal precision. Visible if you have selected "Show Data Labels"
13. **[Color By]** – by "Series order" for unique Color for each series and "Dimension values" by single Color
14. **[Reference Line]** – none, max ten reference lines are allowed. Please refer to page 13 for a detailed explanation.
15. **[Missing Data]** – three options including Line to zero (Default Option), Line breaks, and Linear Interpolation. Please refer to page 9 for a detailed explanation.
16. **[Reverse X and Y-Axis]** – individually or both Axis can be reversed.
17. **[Axis Min and Max and Custom Interval]** – leave to default or area plotted at some point might go above the Axis.
18. **[Custom Interval for Both Axis]** – leave to default Auto. Interval controls the Axis value displayed on both Axis. 7 Interval on X-Axis will have 4 data points for a month and 12 for a year.
19. **[Log Scale]** – Log scales are automatically defined based on the Metrics value and will change both Left Y-Axis and Pub/bar size
20. **[Grid Configuration]** – leave this to default. This will automatically adapt the configurations based on your chart size and color. Consists of Axis Color, Grid Color, Font Family, Font Size, Label Font Size, Chart Backboard, and Border color.
21. **[Background and Border]** – customizable; please refer to page 8 for a detailed explanation.
22. **[Legend]** – the default position is top. Other options are left, bottom, top, and none. Legend alignment (left, centre, right), Legend color, Font Family, Font Size, and Max Lines are also customizable. Please refer to page 13 for a detailed explanation.
23. **[Chart Header]** – chart headers allow viewers to perform several actions on charts, such as data export, drilling up or down, and view charts in explorer tools. Please refer to page 12 for a detailed explanation.

Recommended: Yes, See The Chart Version That Suits Your Need

- **Area Chart 100% Stacking:** If you want to split the trend over time into % share at each interval.
- **Area Chart:** to show the distribution of categories as parts of a whole changing over an interval
- **Area Chart Show Stack:** Same as Area Chart, except in this chart, the smallest series area is plotted on the top rather than bottom.

III. Area Chart: Show Stack

An Area Chart is best used to show the distribution of categories as parts of a whole changing over an interval. As the area inside the chart is plotted to convey whole numbers, an Area Chart does not work for negative values.

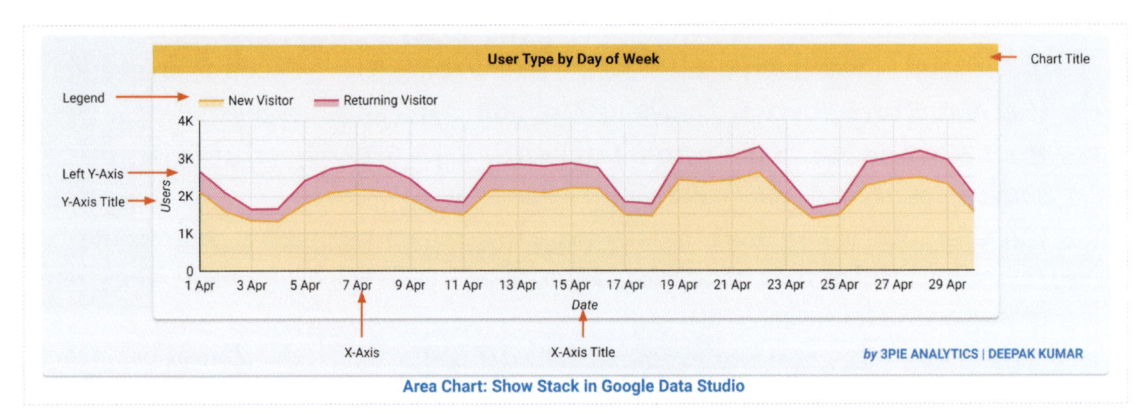

Area Chart: Show Stack in Google Data Studio

- In this chart we display Users Type by weekday, and data is aggregated by weekday for the selected period. The Y-Axis is plotted against the sum on each interval.
- In this chart, the smallest series area is plotted at the top. When hovering over the chart it will display Total Value and raw data for the individual series at each interval.

Chart Configurations:

1. **[Breakdown Dimension]** – Area Chart must have a Breakdown Dimension, selected in the DATA tab, in this example, User Type
2. **[Legend]** – always display legends if your chart has breakdown dimension, Users Type in this example
3. **[Chart Title]** – in an area chart, you have the option to display both Axis together with Legend, and the title is not necessary, but personally, I always prefer to have a title for each chart.
4. **[Data Label]** – not a common practice to display data labels in Area Charts
5. **[X and Y-Axis]** – always display both Axis for an area chart
6. **[X and Y-Axis Title]** – not necessary for area charts, and will save some space for both Axis, especially your chart is small
7. **[Number of Series]** – the number of series in an area chart should be kept moderate as too many series may well hinder its legibility.

Other Configurations: Left To Default

8. **[Show Stack]** – deselecting this option will switch the graph to an Area Chart
9. **[Show Cumulative]** – as a cumulative number

10. **[Show Points]** – add a point on each data point
11. **[Show Data Labels]** – show number at each data point
12. **[Number Format]** – compact Numbers and decimal precision. Visible if you have selected "Show Data Labels"
13. **[Color By]** – by "Series order" for unique Color for each series and "Dimension values" by single Color
14. **[Reference Line]** – none, max ten reference lines are allowed. Please refer to page 13 for a detailed explanation.
15. **[Missing Data]** – three options including Line to zero (Default Option), Line breaks, and Linear Interpolation. Please refer to page 9 for a detailed explanation.
16. **[Reverse X and Y-Axis]** – individually or both Axis can be reversed.
17. **[Axis Min and Max and Custom Interval]** – leave to default or area plotted at some point might go above the Axis.
18. **[Custom Interval for Both Axis]** – leave to default Auto. Interval controls the Axis value displayed on both Axis. 7 Interval on X-Axis will have 4 data points for a month and 12 for a year.
19. **[Log Scale]** – Log scales are automatically defined based on the Metrics value and will change both Left Y-Axis and Pub/bar size
20. **[Grid Configuration]** – leave this to default. This will automatically adapt the configurations based on your chart size and color. Consists of Axis Color, Grid Color, Font Family, Font Size, Label Font Size, Chart Backboard, and Border color:
21. **[Background and Border]** – customizable; please refer to page 8 for a detailed explanation.
22. **[Legend]** – the default position is top. Other options are left, bottom, top, and none. Legend alignment (left, centre, right), Legend color, Font Family, Font Size, and Max Lines are also customizable. Please refer to page 13 for a detailed explanation.
23. **[Chart Header]** – chart headers allow viewers to perform several actions on charts, such as data export, drilling up or down, and view charts in explorer tools. Please refer to page 12 for a detailed explanation.

Recommended: Yes, See The Chart Version That Suits Your Need

- **Area Chart Show Stack:** Same as Area Chart, except in this chart, the smallest series area is plotted on the top rather than bottom.
- **Area Chart:** to show the distribution of categories as parts of a whole changing over an interval
- **Area Chart 100% Stacking:** If you want to split the trend over time into % share at each interval.

Chapter 12: Scatter Charts

A scatter chart will show the relationship between two different variables represented by the X and Y axes.

Use case:

Scatter Chart: to display the relationship between two different variables represented by the X and Y axes.

Recommended: Yes, with one dimension only

It's best to stay one dimensional with both Scatter and Bubble Charts. More than one dimension will be hard to differentiate to most of your report's audience

Scatter Chart in Google Data Studio			
Chart Type	X and Y-Axis	X and Y-Axis Title	Recommended
Scatter Chart with one dimension	Required	Always	Yes
Scatter Chart with two or more dimension	Required	Always	No

Recommended Configurations For Scatter Charts:

1. **[Data Label]** – not a common practice to display data labels in Scatter Charts, but you can display data label if it fits nicely
2. **[Chart Title]** – in a Scatter chart, you have the option to display both Axis together with Legend, and the title is not necessary, but personally, I always prefer to have a title for each chart.
3. **[Number of Bubbles]** – test for the number of bubbles that can fit inside the chart. Too many bubbles will make the chart difficult to read.
4. **[Bubble Color]** – by None and Dimension. If this is left to None, Bubble color will be the same for all dimensions variable and individual Bubble color if selected Dimension.
5. **[X and Y-Axis]** – both Axis must have a metric in a Scatter Chart selected in the DATA tab and always display both Axis for a Scatter Chart
6. **[X and Y-Axis Title]** – display both Axis titles in a Scatter Chart so the audience can quickly identify metrics displayed on each Axis
7. **[Grid]** – adding a grid will help identify the metric values on both Axes quickly.
8. **[Legend]** – a Legend will be displayed based on Bubble color configuration. If we choose to select None, the Bubble Color for each variable will be the same

Others Configurations Available Within Scatter Charts:

9. **[Reference Line]** – none, max ten reference lines are allowed. Please refer to page 13 for a detailed explanation.
10. **[Missing Data]** – three options including Line to zero (Default Option), Line breaks, and Linear Interpolation. Please refer to page 9 for a detailed explanation.
11. **[Reverse X and Y-Axis]** – individually or both Axis can be reversed.
12. **[Axis Min and Max and Custom Interval]** – leave to default or area plotted at some point might go above the Axis.
13. **[Custom Interval for Both Axis]** – leave to default Auto. Interval controls the Axis value displayed on both Axis. 7 Interval on X-Axis will have 4 data points for a month and 12 for a year.
14. **[Log Scale]** – Log scales are automatically defined based on the Metrics value and will change both Left Y-Axis and Pub/bar size
15. **[Grid Configuration]** – leave this to default. This will automatically adapt the configurations based on your chart size and color. Consists of Axis Color, Grid Color, Font Family, Font Size, Label Font Size, Chart Backboard, and Border color.
16. **[Background Color, Border Radius, and Opacity]** – customizable; please refer to page 8 for a detailed explanation.
17. **[Border Color, Weight, and Style]** – customizable; please refer to page 8 for a detailed explanation.
18. **[Legend]** – The default position is top. Other options are left, bottom, top, and none. Legend alignment (left, centre, right), Legend color, Font Family, Font Size, and Max Lines are also customizable. Please refer to page 13 for a detailed explanation.
19. **[Chart Header]** – chart headers allow viewers to perform several actions on charts, such as data export, drilling up or down, and view charts in explorer tools. Please refer to page 12 for a detailed explanation.

I. Scatter Chart

A scatter chart will show the relationship between two different variables represented by the X and Y axes.

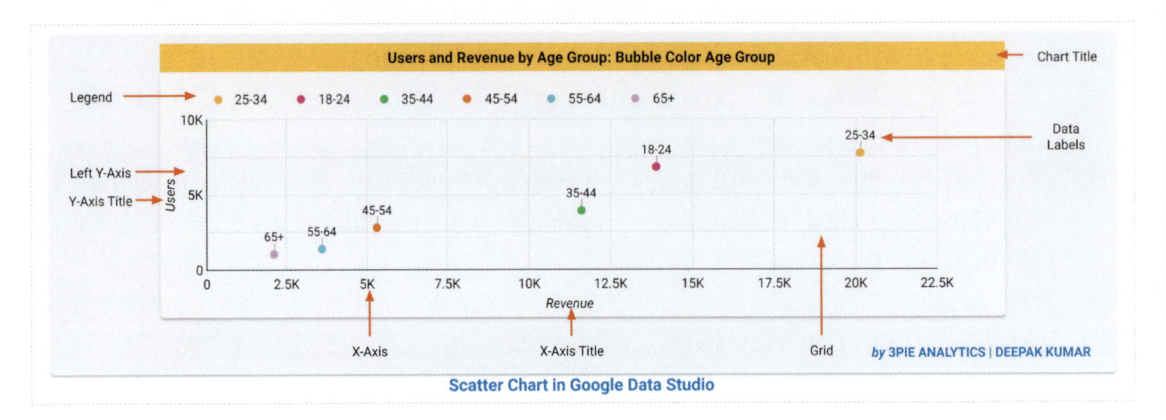

Scatter Chart in Google Data Studio

- In this chart we are displaying Users and Revenue by Age Group for the selected time range.

Chart Configurations:

1. **[Data Label]** – not a common practice to display data labels in Scatter Charts, but you can display data label if it fits nicely
2. **[Chart Title]** – in a Scatter chart, you have the option to display both Axis together with Legend, and the title is not necessary, but personally, I always prefer to have a title for each chart.
3. **[Number of Bubbles]** – test for the number of bubbles that can fit inside the chart. Too many bubbles will make the chart difficult to read.
4. **[Bubble Color]** – includes None and by Dimension. If this is left to None, Bubble color will be the same for each age group in the above example.
5. **[X and Y-Axis]** – both Axis must have a metric in a Scatter Chart selected in the DATA tab and always display both Axis for a Scatter Chart
6. **[X and Y-Axis Title]** – display both Axis titles in a Scatter Chart so the audience can quickly identify metrics displayed on each Axis
7. **[Grid]** – adding a grid will help identify the metric values on both Axes quickly. In this example, the 25-34 age group generated around 20k revenue from around 7.5k Users.
8. **[Legend]** – a Legend will be displayed based on Bubble color configuration. In this example we have selected Age. If we choose to select None, the Legend will be "Age" instead of "Age Group" and will be the same Bubble Color for each Age Group.

Other Configurations: Left To Default

9. **[Reference Line]** – none, max ten reference lines are allowed. Please refer to page 13 for a detailed explanation.
    a. **[Reference Line Type - Metrics]** – calculation includes Average, Median, Percentile, Min, Max, and Total. Reference line will be automatically created based on the Metrics value
    b. **[Reference Line Type - Constant value]** – a custom number that is to be displayed on the Left or Right Y-Axis
    c. **[Reference Line Type - Parameter]** – if you have set a Parameter in your report
    d. **[Reference Line - Label]** – customizable, you can assign Reference Line name to your desired name.
    e. **[Reference Line - Color]** – customizable; you can assign a custom color.
10. **[Missing Data]** – three options including Line to zero (Default Option), Line breaks, and Linear Interpolation
11. **[Reverse X and Y-Axis]** – individually or both Axis can be reversed. If we reverse the X-Axis for the above chart, Saturday will show first instead of Sunday
12. **[Axis Min and Max and Custom Interval]** – leave to default or area plotted at some point might go above the Axis.
13. **[Custom Interval for Both Axis]** – leave to default Auto. Interval controls the Axis value displayed on both. 7 Interval on X-Axis will have 7 Apr as a second date point instead of 3 Apr in the above chart
14. **[Log Scale]** – Log scales are automatically defined based on the Metrics value and will change both Left Y-Axis and Pub/bar size
15. **[Grid Configuration]** – leave this to default. This will automatically adapt the configurations based on your chart size and color. Consists of Axis Color, Grid Color, Font Family, Font Size, Label Font Size, Chart Backboard, and Border color.
16. **[Background Color, Border Radius, and Opacity]** – customizable; please refer to page 8 for a detailed explanation.
17. **[Border Color, Weight, and Style]** – customizable; please refer to page 8 for a detailed explanation.
18. **[Legend]** – the default position is top. Other options are left, bottom, top, and none. Legend alignment (left, centre, right), Legend color, Font Family, Font Size, and Max Lines are also customizable. Please refer to page 13 for a detailed explanation.
19. **[Chart Header]** – chart headers allow viewers to perform several actions on charts, such as data export, drilling up or down, and view charts in explorer tools. Please refer to page 12 for a detailed explanation.

Recommended: Yes, With One Dimension

- It's best to stay one dimensional with both Scatter and Bubble Charts. More than one dimension will be hard to differentiate to most of your report's audience – see next example

II. Scatter Chart: Two or more Dimensions

A scatter chart will show the relationship between two different variables represented by the X and Y axes.

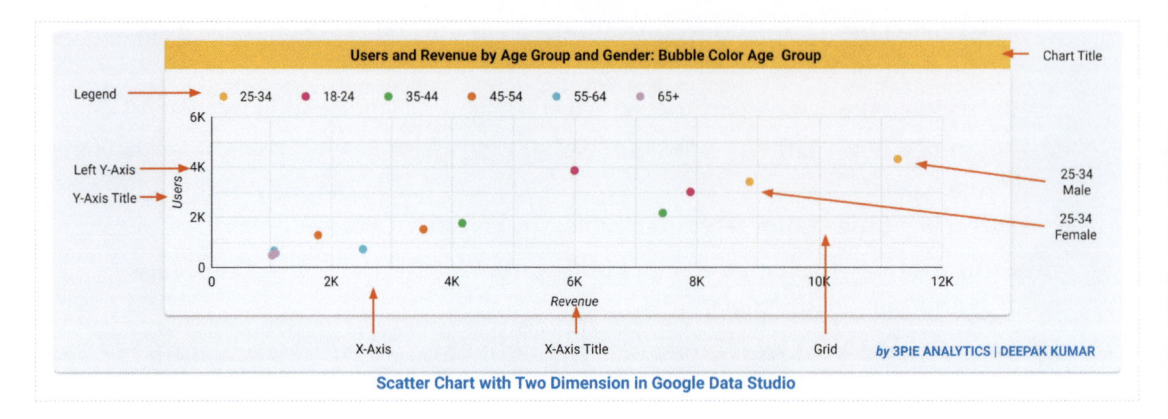

Scatter Chart with Two Dimension in Google Data Studio

- In this chart, we are displaying Users and Revenue by age Group. Bubble Size (Optional) representing Revenue per user
1. **[Grid]** – adding a grid will help identify the metric values on both Axes quickly. In this example, the 25-34 age group generated around 11k revenue from around 4.1k Users.
2. **[Legend]** – a Legend will be displayed based on Bubble color configuration. In this example we have selected Age. If we choose to select None, the Legend will be "Age" instead of "Age Group" and will be the same Bubble Color for each Age Group.

Recommended: No

No, unless it's absolutely necessary. In general, you should avoid having Scatter and Bubble charts with two dimensions as it will be hard to differentiate to most of your report's audience.

Left empty for two page configuration

Chapter 13: Bubble Chart = Scatter Chart + Bubble Size

A Bubble chart shows the relationship between two different variables represented by the X and Y axes, with Bubble Size (optional) representing Revenue per user.

Use case:

Bubble Chart: to display the relationship between two different variables represented by the X and Y axes. Bubble Size (optional) to represent the relative size of the metrics values

Recommended: Yes, with one dimension only

It's best to stay one dimensional with both Bubble and Scatter Charts. More than one dimension will be hard to differentiate to most of your report's audience

\multicolumn{4}{c	}{Bubble Chart in Google Data Studio}
Chart Type	X and Y-Axis	X and Y-Axis Title	Recommended
Bubble Chart with one dimension	Required	Always	Yes
Bubble Chart with two or more dimension	Required	Always	No

Recommended Configurations For Bubble Charts:

1. **[Data Label]** – not a common practice to display data labels in Scatter Charts, but you can display data label if it fits nicely
2. **[Chart Title]** – in a Bubble chart, you have the option to display both Axis together with Legend, and the title is not necessary, but personally, I always prefer to have a title for each chart.
3. **[Bubble Size]** – optional metrics are selected in the DATA tab; if left empty, this will be Scatter Chart shown in the previous chapter. Bubble size adjustable with slide
4. **[Number of Bubbles]** – test for the number of bubbles that can fit inside the chart. Too many bubbles will make the chart difficult to read.
5. **[Bubble Color]** – by None and Dimension. If this is left to None, Bubble color will be the same for all dimensions variable and individual Bubble color if selected Dimension.
6. **[Color by]** – default by "Bubble order" and by "Dimension value"

7. **[Number of Bubbles]** – default is 1000. Test for the number bubble that can fit inside the chart, and too many bubbles will make the chart difficult to read.
8. **[X and Y-Axis]** – both X and Y-Axis must have a metric in a Bubble Chart and always display both Axis for a Bubble Chart.
9. **[X and Y-Axis Title]** – display both Axis titles in a bubble Chart so the audience can quickly identify metrics displayed on each Axis
10. **[Grid]** – adding a grid will help identify metrics value on both Axes quickly.
11. **[Legend]** – a Legend will be displayed based on Bubble color configuration. If we choose to select None, the Bubble Color for each variable will be the same

Others Configurations Available Within Bubble Charts:

12. **[Reference Line]** – none, max ten reference lines are allowed. Please refer to page 13 for a detailed explanation.
13. **[Reverse X and Y-Axis]** – individually or both Axis can be reversed. If we reverse the X-Axis for the above chart, Saturday will show first instead of Sunday
14. **[Axis Min and Max value]** – leave to default or bubble might go above the Axis.
15. **[Custom Interval for Both Axis]** – leave to default Auto. Interval controls the Axis value displayed on both Axis. 7 Interval on X-Axis will have 4 data points for a month and 12 for a year.
16. **[Log Scale]** – Log scales are automatically defined based on the Metrics value and will change both Left Y-Axis and Pub/bar size
17. **[Grid Configuration]** – leave this to default. This will automatically adapt the configurations based on your chart size and color. Consists of Axis Color, Grid Color, Font Family, Font Size, Label Font Size, Chart Backboard, and Border color.
18. **[Background Color, Border Radius, and Opacity]** – customizable; please refer to page 8 for a detailed explanation.
19. **[Border Color, Weight, and Style]** – customizable; please refer to page 8 for a detailed explanation.
20. **[Legend]** – the default position is top. Other options are left, bottom, top, and none. Legend alignment (left, centre, right), Legend color, Font Family, Font Size, and Max Lines are also customizable. Please refer to page 13 for a detailed explanation.
21. **[Chart Header]** – chart headers allow viewers to perform several actions on charts, such as data export, drilling up or down, and view charts in explorer tools. Please refer to page 12 for a detailed explanation.

I. Bubble Chart = Scatter Chart + Bubble Size Configuration

A Bubble chart shows the relationship between two different variables represented by the X and Y axes, with Bubble Size (optional) representing Revenue per user.

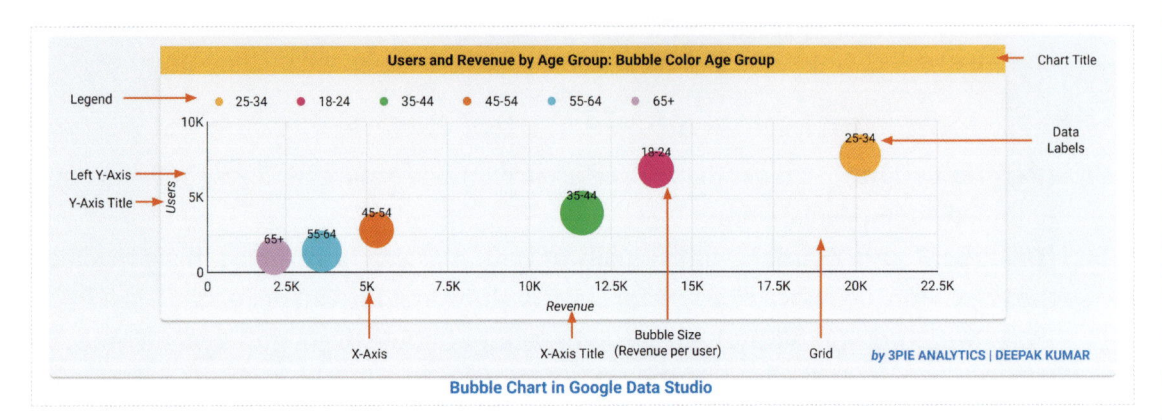

Bubble Chart in Google Data Studio

– In this chart, we are displaying Users and Revenue by Age Group, with Bubble Size (optional) representing Revenue per user. Without the Bubble Size configuration, the above chart would be a Scatter Chart.

Chart Configurations:

1. **[Data Label]** – not a common practice to display data labels in Scatter Charts, but you can display data label if it fits nicely
2. **[Chart Title]** – in a Bubble chart, you have the option to display both Axis together with Legend, and the title is not necessary, but personally, I always prefer to have a title for each chart.
3. **[Bubble Size]** – optional metrics are selected in the DATA tab; if left empty, this will be Scatter Chart shown in the previous chapter. Bubble size adjustable with slide
4. **[Number of Bubbles]** – test for the number of bubbles that can fit inside the chart. Too many bubbles will make the chart difficult to read.
5. **[Bubble Color]** – default by None and by Dimension. If this is left to None, Bubble color will be the same for each age group in the above example.
6. **[Color by]** – default by "Bubble order" other by "Dimension value"
7. **[Number of Bubbles]** – default is 1000. Test for the number bubble that can fit inside the chart, and too many bubbles will make the chart difficult to read.
8. **[X and Y-Axis]** – both X and Y-Axis must have a metric in a Bubble Chart and always display both Axis for a Bubble Chart.

9. **[X and Y-Axis Title]** – display both Axis titles in a bubble Chart so the audience can quickly identify metrics displayed on each Axis
10. **[Grid]** – adding a grid will help identify metrics value on both Axes quickly. In this example, the 25-34 age group generated around 20k Revenue from around 7.5k Users.
11. **[Legend]** – a Legend will be displayed based on Bubble Color configuration. In this example we have selected Age. If we choose to select None, the Legend will be "Age" instead of each Age Group. Bubble Color will be the same for every Age Group.

Other Configurations:

12. **[Reference Line]** – none, max ten reference lines are allowed. Please refer to page 13 for a detailed explanation.
13. **[Reverse X and Y-Axis]** – individually or both Axis can be reversed. If we reverse the X-Axis for the above chart, Saturday will show first instead of Sunday
14. **[Axis Min and Max and Custom Interval]** – leave to default or bubble might go above the Axis.
15. **[Custom Interval for Both Axis]** – leave to default Auto. Interval controls the Axis value displayed on both. 7 Interval on X-Axis will have 7 Apr as a second date point instead of 3 Apr in the above chart
16. **[Log Scale]** – Log scales are automatically defined based on the Metrics value and will change both Left Y-Axis and Pub/bar size
17. **[Grid Configuration]** – leave this to default. This will automatically adapt the configurations based on your chart size and color. Consists of Axis Color, Grid Color, Font Family, Font Size, Label Font Size, Chart Backboard, and Border color.
18. **[Background Color, Border Radius, and Opacity]** – customizable; please refer to page 8 for a detailed explanation.
19. **[Border Color, Weight, and Style]** – customizable; please refer to page 8 for a detailed explanation.
20. **[Legend]** – The default position is top. Other options are left, bottom, top, and none. Legend alignment (left, centre, right), Legend color, Font Family, Font Size, and Max Lines are also customizable. Please refer to page 13 for a detailed explanation.
21. **[Chart Header]** – chart headers allow viewers to perform several actions on charts, such as data export, drilling up or down, and view charts in explorer tools. Please refer to page 12 for a detailed explanation.

Recommended: Yes, With One Dimension

- It's best to stay one dimensional with both Scatter and Bubble Charts. More than one dimension will be hard to differentiate to most of your report's audience – see next example.

II. Bubble Chart: Two or more Dimensions

A Bubble chart shows the relationship between two different variables represented by the X and Y axes, with Bubble Size (optional) representing Revenue per user.

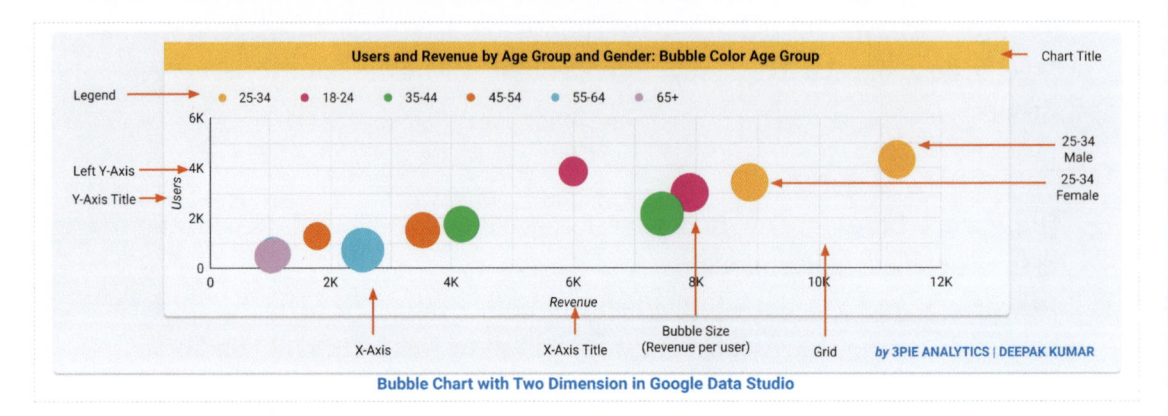

Bubble Chart with Two Dimension in Google Data Studio

- In this chart, we are displaying Users and Revenue by Age Group, with Bubble Size (optional) representing Revenue per user. Without the Bubble Size configuration, the above chart would be a Scatter Chart.

Recommended: No

- As you can see, we have two same colors for each age group, and unless we have data labels, it's hard to differentiate. But, unfortunately, the data labels will make the chart very messy in most cases.

Chapter 14: Geo Maps Charts

Geo charts are an easy way to visualize data in maps to compare how a measurement varies across a geographic area. The dimensions are related to continents, countries, regions/states and cities, with your desired metrics as a data point.

Use case:

1. **Geo Chart [a personal favorite]:** Chart areas are color-filled based on High, Medium, Low and data less values. A Geo Chart only has the option to set Zoom Area.
2. **Bubble Map:** Chart areas are filled as Bubbles and the chart has an option to display as a Map or Satellite view. Bubble maps have two background layer options (map or satellite views) which can be configured in the Style Tab. You can also set the number of Bubbles and the Bubbles Size.
3. **Filled Map:** Almost the same as Geo chart, except the there is no option to set the Zoom area. Filled maps have two background layer options (map and satellite views) which can be configured in the Style Tab.

Recommended: Yes, see the chart version that suits your need

Geo Chart in Google Data Studio			
Chart Type	X and Y-Axis	X and Y-Axis Title	Recommended
Geo Chart	Optional	Always	Yes, personal favorite
Bubble Map	Optional	Always	Yes
Filled Map	Optional	Always	Yes

Recommended Configurations Across Geo Map Charts:

1. **[Geo Dimension]** – must be a geo-location dimension
2. **[Chart Title]** – Filled map chart is self-explanatory, but for the metrics, I prefer to have a title to show the data represented in a Geo chart
3. **[Background Layer Type]** – choose between Map or Satellite View
4. **[Legend]** – it's best practice to display the Legend which provides the maximum value for the dimension
5. **[Filled Color]** – chart areas are filled based on High, Medium, Low, and Dataless values. Filled color can be also configured in the STYLE tab

6. **[Report Theme]** – default silver,, Standards, Dark, and Custom JSON.

Geo Chart Only:

7. **[Zoom Area]** – Geo Chart only has an option to set Zoom Area.

Filed Map Only:

8. **[Metric #]** – A Filled Map can only have one Metric

Bubble And Filled Map Only:

9. **[Tooltip]** – optional - a tooltip lets the user override the default label provided by the location dimension. For example, you could use bubbles based on store addresses, but use the store name in the Tooltip. Note, Tooltip dimension must have a unique value for each location, or your chart will show an error.
10. **Background Style Configuration:**
    i) **[Roads]** – this can turn off and off. Roads are shown in the above example
    ii) **[Landmarks]** – this can turn off and off. Landmarks are shown in the above example
    iii) **[Labels]** – this can turn off and off. Labels (Country) are shown in the above example
11. **[Layer Type]** – choose between Filled Area or Bubble. Changing to Bubble in the above example will switch to a Bubble Chart
12. **[Filled Area Layer]** – Opacity: Bubble Color Capacity, default is set to 50%; Border Weight: Default set to None
13. **[Filled Color]** – chart areas are filled based on High, Medium, Low, and Dataless values.
14. **Map Controls: Can be turned Off or ON**
    i) **Allow pan and zoom:** Move the chart area mouse point. Default Selected
    ii) **Show zoom control:** Plus and Minus in the above chart (Right Side). Default Selected
    iii) **Show Street View control:** Human icon. Default Selected
    iv) **Show fullscreen control:** Square (Top Right). Default Selected
    v) **Show map type control:** Map and Satellite (Top Left)
    vi) **Show scale control:** Bottom Right Scale in the above chart
15. **Color Legend:**
    i) **Position:** None (Default), Bottom, Top, Left, and Right
    ii) **Alignment:** Left (Default), Center, and Right
    iii) **Max Line:** Number of lines
    iv) **Legend Title:** Font Color, Font Color, and Font
    v) Compact Number and Decimal Precision

Others Configurations Available Within Geo Maps Charts:

16. **[Background Border and Chart Header]** – Please refer to page 8 for a detailed explanation.

I. Geo Chart

Geo charts are an easy way to visualize data in maps to compare how a measurement varies across a geographic area. The dimensions are related to continents, countries, regions/states and cities, with your desired metrics as a data point.

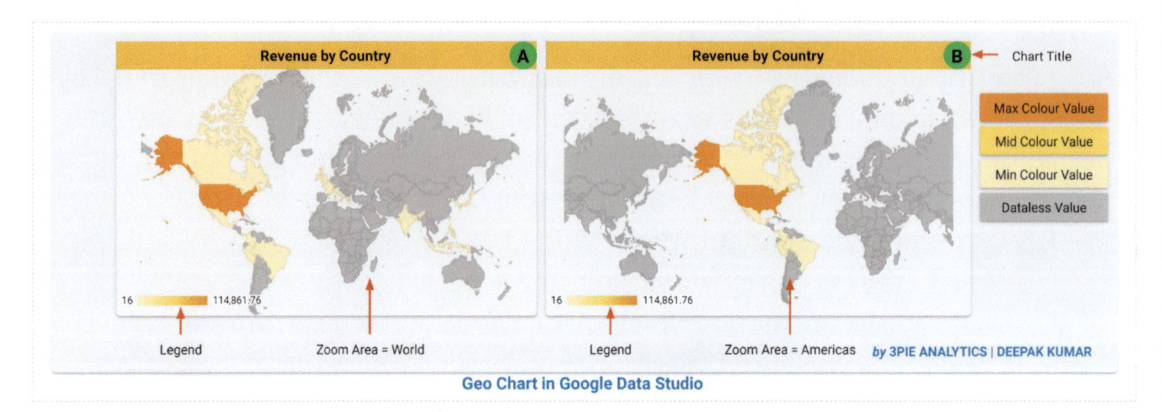

Geo Chart in Google Data Studio

- In this chart, we are displaying Revenue by Country.
- In Chart A, Zoom Area is set to default as World, and in Chart B, Zoom Area is set to Americas.

Chart Configurations:

1. **[Geo Dimension]** – must be a geo-location dimension
2. **[Chart Title]** – Geo chart is self-explanatory, but for the metrics, I prefer to have a title to show the data represented in a Geo chart
3. **[Legend]** – it's best practice to display the Legend which provides the maximum value for the dimension
4. **[Filled Color]** – chart areas are filled based on High, Medium, Low, and Dataless values. Filled color can be configured in the STYLE tab
5. **[Zoom Area]** – Geo Chart only has an option to set Zoom Area. In this example, Zoom Area is set to Americas
6. **[Font]** – Theme default Roboto in the above example

Other Configurations: Left To Default

7. **[Background Color, Border Radius, and Opacity]** – customizable; please refer to page 8 for a detailed explanation.
8. **[Border Color, Weight, and Style]** – customizable; please refer to page 8 for a detailed explanation.
9. **[Chart Header]** – chart headers allow viewers to perform several actions on charts, such as data export, drilling up or down, and view charts in explorer tools. Please refer to page 12 for a detailed explanation.

Recommended: Yes, See The Chart Version That Suits Your Need

- **Geo Chart [a personal favorite]:** Chart areas are color-filled based on High, Medium, Low and data less values. A Geo Chart only has the option to set Zoom Area.
- **Bubble Map:** Chart areas are filled as Bubbles and the chart has an option to display as a Map or Satellite view. Bubble maps have two background layer options (map or satellite views) which can be configured in the Style Tab. You can also set the number of Bubbles and the Bubbles Size.
- **Filled Map:** Almost the same as Geo chart, except the there is no option to set the Zoom area. Filled maps have two background layer options (map and satellite views) which can be configured in the Style Tab.

II. Filled Map

Filled map charts provide an easy way to visualize your data in maps and compare how a measurement varies across a geographic area. The dimensions are related to continents, countries, regions/states and cities, with your desired metrics as a data point.

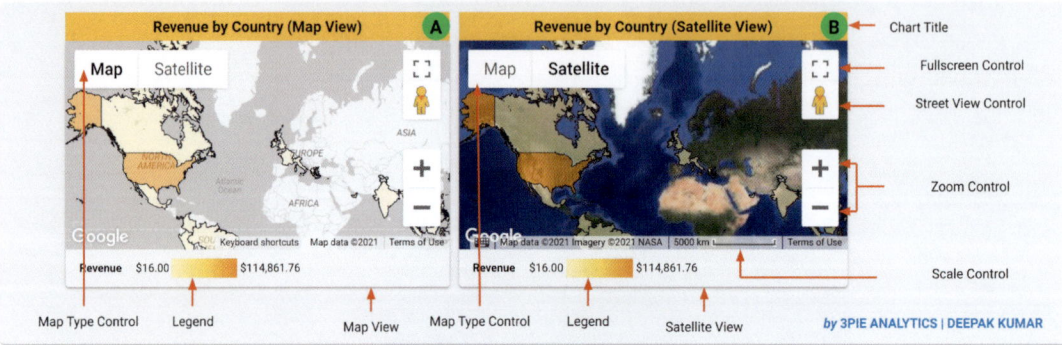

Filled Map Chart in Google Data Studio

- A Filled Map can only have one Metric. In this chart, we are displaying Revenue by Country. Chart A Map View and Chart B Satellite View.

Chart Configurations:

1. **[Chart Title]** – Filled map chart is self-explanatory, but for the metrics, I prefer to have a title to show the data represented in a Geo chart
2. **[Legend]** – it's best practice to display the Legend, which provides the minimum and maximum value for the dimension
3. **[Tooltip]** – Optional - a tooltip lets the user override the default label provided by the location dimension. For example, you could use bubbles based on store addresses, but use the store name in the Tooltip. Note, Tooltip dimension must have a unique value for each location, or your chart will show an error.
4. **[Background Layer Type]** – choose between Map or Satellite View
5. **[Report Theme]** – default silver, other options include, Standards, Dark and Custom JSON.

Background Style Configuration:

1. **[Roads]** – this can turn off and off. Roads are shown in the above example
2. **[Landmarks]** – this can turn off and off. Landmarks are shown in the above example
3. **[Labels]** – this can turn off and off. Labels (Country) are shown in the above example

4. **[Layer Type]** – choose between Filled Area or Bubble. Changing to Bubble in the above example will switch to a Bubble Chart
5. **[Filled Area Layer]** – Opacity: Bubble Color Capacity, default is set to 50%; Border Weight: Default set to None
6. **[Filled Color]** – chart areas are filled based on High, Medium, Low, and Dataless values.

Map Controls: Can Be Turned Off Or On

1. **Allow pan and zoom:** Move the chart area mouse point. Default Selected
2. **Show zoom control:** Plus and Minus in the above chart (Right Side). Default Selected
3. **Show Street View control:** Human icon. Default Selected
4. **Show fullscreen control:** Square (Top Right). Default Selected
5. **Show map type control:** Map and Satellite (Top Left)
6. **Show scale control:** Bottom Right Scale in the above chart

Color Legend:

1. **Position:** None (Default), Bottom, Top, Left, and Right
2. **Alignment:** Left (Default), Center, and Right
3. **Max Line:** Number of lines
4. **Legend Title:** Font Color, Font Color, and Font
5. Compact Number and Decimal Precision

Other Configurations: Left To Default

1. **[Background and Border]** – customizable; please refer to page 8 for a detailed explanation.
2. **[Chart Header]** – chart headers allow viewers to perform several actions on charts, such as data export, drilling up or down, and view charts in explorer tools. Please refer to page 12 for a detailed explanation.

Recommended: Yes, See The Chart Version That Suits Your Need

- **Filled Map:** Almost the same as Geo chart, except the there is no option to set the Zoom area. Filled maps have two background layer options (map and satellite views) which can be configured in the Style Tab.
- **Geo Chart [a personal favorite]:** Chart areas are color-filled based on High, Medium, Low and data less values. A Geo Chart only has the option to set Zoom Area.
- **Bubble Map:** Chart areas are filled as Bubbles and the chart has an option to display as a Map or Satellite view. Bubble maps have two background layer options (map or satellite views) which can be configured in the Style Tab. You can also set the number of Bubbles and the Bubbles Size

III. Bubble Map

Bubble map charts provide an easy way to visualize your data in maps and compare how a measurement varies across a geographic area. The dimensions are related to continents, countries, regions/states and cities, with your desired metrics as data points.

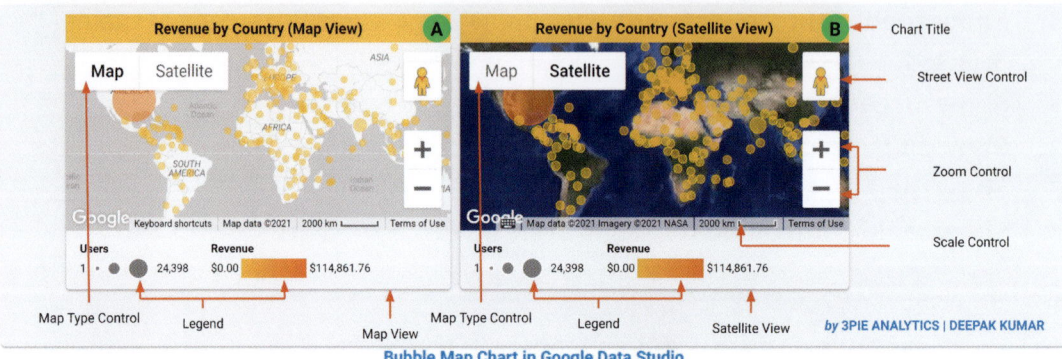

Bubble Map Chart in Google Data Studio

- In this chart, we are displaying Users (Size) and Revenue (Color) by Country.
- Bubble map has two Metrics options, Size and Color, and possible to use one either of them.
- Chart A Map View and Chart B Satellite View.

Chart Configurations:

1. **[Chart Title]** – title is not necessary for a bubble chart. Personally, I always prefer to have a title for each chart.
2. **[Legend]** – it's best practice to display the Legend, which provides the minimum and maximum value for the dimension
3. **[Tooltip]** – Optional - a tooltip lets the user override the default label provided by the location dimension. For example, you could use bubbles based on store addresses, but use the store name in the Tooltip. Note, Tooltip dimension must have a unique value for each location, or your chart will show an error.
4. **[Background Layer Type]** – choose between Map or Satellite View
5. **[Report Theme]** – default silver, other options include, Standards, Dark and Custom JSON.
6. **Background Style Configuration:**
    i) **[Roads]** – this can turn off and off. Roads are shown in the above example
    ii) **[Landmarks]** – this can turn off and off. Landmarks are shown in the above example
    iii) **[Labels]** – this can turn off and off. Labels (Country) are shown in the above example

7. **[Layer Type]** – choose between Filled Area or Bubble. Changing to Area in the above example will switch to an Area Chart.
8. **[Bubble Layer]** – Opacity: Bubble Color Capacity, default is set to 50%; Border Weight: Default set to None
9. **[Filled Color]** – chart areas are filled based on High, Medium, Low, and Dataless values.

Map Controls: Can Be Turned Off Or On

1. **Allow pan and zoom:** Move the chart area mouse point. Default Selected
2. **Show zoom control:** Plus and Minus in the above chart (Right Side). Default Selected
3. **Show Street View control:** Human icon. Default Selected
4. **Show fullscreen control:** Square (Top Right). Default Selected
5. **Show map type control:** Map and Satellite (Top Left)
6. **Show scale control:** Bottom Right Scale in the above chart

Color Legend:

1. **Position:** None (Default), Bottom, Top, Left, and Right
2. **Alignment:** Left (Default), Center, and Right
3. **Max Line:** Number of lines
4. **Legend Title:** Font Color, Font Color, and Font
5. Compact Number and Decimal Precision

Other Configurations: Left To Default

1. **[Background and Border]** – customizable; please refer to page 8 for a detailed explanation.
2. **[Chart Header]** – chart headers allow viewers to perform several actions on charts, such as data export, drilling up or down, and view charts in explorer tools. Please refer to page 12 for a detailed explanation.

Recommended: Yes, See The Chart Version That Suits Your Need

- **Bubble Map:** Chart areas are filled as Bubbles and the chart has an option to display as a Map or Satellite view. Bubble maps have two background layer options (map or satellite views) which can be configured in the Style Tab. You can also set the number of Bubbles and the Bubbles Size.
- **Filled Map:** Almost the same as Geo chart, except the there is no option to set the Zoom area. Filled maps have two background layer options (map and satellite views) which can be configured in the Style Tab.
- **Geo Chart [a personal favorite]:** Chart areas are color-filled based on High, Medium, Low and data less values. A Geo Chart only has the option to set Zoom Area.

Chapter 15: Treemap

Treemaps show parts of a whole and display hierarchical information.

Recommended: Yes, with a single dimension

Treemap Chart in Google Data Studio			
Chart Type	Chart Title	Filled Color	Recommended
Treemap Chart: single dimension	Optional	Always	Yes
Treemap Chart: two or more dimension	Optional	Always	Yes

Recommended Configurations For Treemap Charts:

1. **[Chart Title]** – not necessary, but personally, I always prefer to have a title for each Chart.
2. **[Filled Color]** – chart areas are filled based on High, Medium, Min values. Filled color can be configured in the STYLE tab
3. **[Branch Header]** – best practice to display if you have more than one Metrics.

Others Configurations Available Within Treemap Charts:

4. **[Branch Header color]** – default blue
5. **[Text]:** Font Color, Font Size, and Font Family
6. **[Levels to show]** – configured in the DATA tab, this controls the number of Branch headers to show
7. **[Total Rows]** – data Points to show within the Chart, excluding the headers. Configured in the DATA tab
8. **[Dimension Label]** – displayed natively in Treemap charts and no option to hide or show. Country name in the above example
9. **[Background Color, Border Radius, and Opacity]** – customizable; please refer to page 8 for a detailed explanation.
10. **[Border Color, Weight, and Style]** – customizable; please refer to page 8 for a detailed explanation.
11. **[Chart Header]** – chart headers allow viewers to perform several actions on charts, such as data export, drilling up or down, and view charts in explorer tools. Please refer to page 12 for a detailed explanation.

I. Treemap Chart

Treemaps show parts of a whole and display hierarchical information.

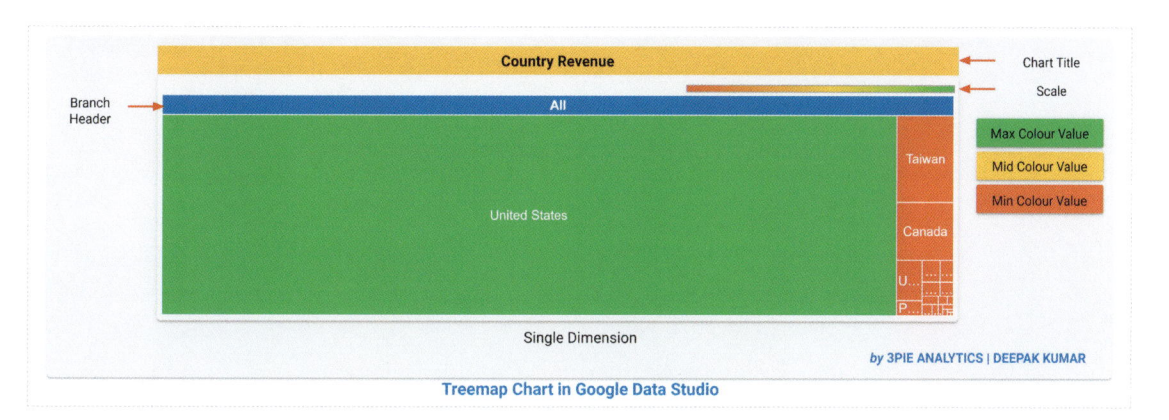

Treemap Chart in Google Data Studio

– In this chart we are displaying County and Gender Revenue.

Chart Configurations:

1. **[Chart Title]** – not necessary, but personally, I always prefer to have a title for each Chart.
2. **[Filled Color]** – chart areas are filled based on High, Medium, Min values. Filled color can be configured in the STYLE tab
3. **[Branch Header]** – best practice to display if you have more than one Metrics (Next Chart)

Other Configurations: Left To Default

4. **[Branch Header color]** – default blue
5. **[Text]** – Font Color, Font Size, and Font Family
6. **[Levels to show]** – configured in the DATA tab, this controls the number of Branch headers to show
7. **[Total Rows]** – data Points to show within the Chart, excluding the headers. Configured in the DATA tab
8. **[Dimension Label]** – displayed natively in Treemap charts and no option to hide or show. Country name in the above example
9. **[Background and Border]** – customizable; please refer to page 8 for a detailed explanation.
10. **[Chart Header]** – chart headers allow viewers to perform several actions on charts, such as data export, drilling up or down, and view charts in explorer tools. Please refer to page 12 for a detailed explanation.

Recommended: Yes, With A Single Dimension Configuration

II. Treemap Chart – Two or more dimension

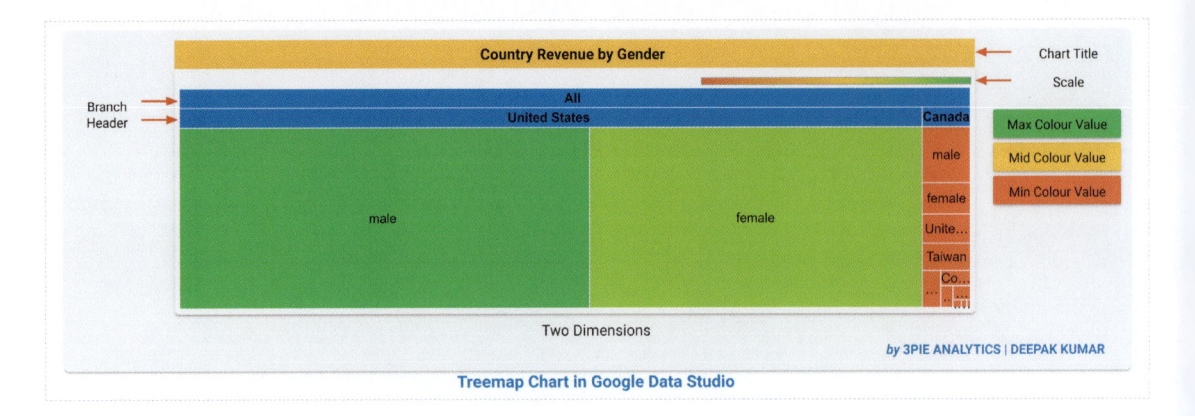

- In this chart we are displaying County and Gender Revenue.

Recommended: No

- In this example, over 90% of revenue is coming from the US. While the Chart looks excellent, a treemap can be difficult to visualize in two dimensions. Avoid having two dimensions unless it's absolutely necessary. If you have to use this Chart, test the number of rows that can fit nicely inside your graph and display the Chart on the full-width page.